ALGONQUIN PARK

proper spelling Algonkin; Haliburton county. A word of
unknown etymology. It is the name of a great tribe of
Indians who lived north of Lake Superior and Lake
Huron and on the east to the Ottawa River. The word
means 'spearing fish from the end of a canoe'.

FROM THE BOOK, 'INDIAN PLACE NAMES IN ONTARIO'
by Capt. W. F. Moore
The MacMillan Company, 1930.

ALONG THE TRAIL
with Ralph Bice
IN ALGONQUIN PARK

CONSOLIDATED AMETHYST

Canadian Cataloguing in Publication Data
Bice, Ralph, 1900
Penhale, Barry Lloyd, Editor, 1932
ALONG THE TRAIL
WITH RALPH BICE IN ALGONQUIN PARK
Text in English
I. Elphick, John   II. Title
All Rights Reserved
© COPYRIGHT 1980
by Consolidated Amethyst Communications Inc.

ISBN 0-920474-19-5

Consolidated Amethyst Communications Inc.
60 Barbados Boulevard, Unit 6,
Scarborough, Ontario M1J 1K9

1st Printing — August 1980

Contents

This book is lovingly dedicated to the memory of the many, many friends I have made in the almost seventy years I have spent in Algonquin Park. Guides, Rangers, cottagers, hotel staff and others, all who helped to make summers such a pleasant time of the year. More especially to those members of my own family who have passed on; my grandfather, my father, my son, my two brothers, and uncles, all who have enjoyed the peace and beauty of the Park, and whose friendship brings back so many pleasant memories. Since they all enjoyed the quite and serenity of those beauties the Park supplied, I can only ask:

Semper per haec colles et lacusaque errant.

By these hills and waters may they ever roam.

A winter timber hauling operation.

The Publisher
is grateful to the following
for their
interest and cooperation
concerning the publication
of this book

The Hon. Frank Miller
The Hon. James A. C. Auld
Dr. J. Keith Reynolds
Mr. W.T. (Bill) Foster
and the many others with
the Ontario Ministry of Natural Resources
who consider Ralph Bice
a nice person to know.

At the end of a portage in 1897.

Introduction

I am honoured to have been asked to write this introduction to a history of one man's special relationship with one of Ontario's great institutions.

Ralph Bice, about whose life and experiences this book is written, is a man I have come to know both in my official capacities over the years and as an ordinary citizen living in close proximity to Algonquin Park. Indeed, to many people living near the Park, the name Ralph Bice is synonymous with Algonquin Park. I consider him a friend, and though he from time to time will remind us in government of our occasional inattention to the nurturing of this great resource, I have learned to value his insights into the Park specifically, and the out-doors generally.

The creation and preservation of this park is a tribute to the foresight of the people of Ontario. A significant recreational area of some 2,910 square miles, it was our first provincial park; even today, it ranks among the country's largest parks. Located on the fringes of the Canadian Shield, Algonquin has long been noted for its intriguing mixture of wildlife and vegetation because of its transitional situation. Its lasting beauty is a tremendous asset to this Province, making it an attraction that can be treasured for generations.

The park region has an interesting history. The effects of glaciation are still evident; large deposits of sand and gravel were left and thousands of lakes were carved out. Arctic tundra plants developed, followed by the growth of pine and spruce. The area was relatively untouched by man until the 1850's. At that time, pioneer loggers in search of giant white pine swept into the region. The timber was increasingly in demand by the British economy and woodsmen felled the enormous conifers, squared the trunks, and drove them off to the Ottawa River for processing.

Supplies, however, began to dwindle as more men pushed further into the interior and in 1893, by the time the Park was established, most of the pine had been cut or fire-ravaged. A wildlife sanctuary was created and agricultural development prohibited, which also protected the headwaters of five major rivers that flow from the area.

Logging has continued to play an important role in the region's economic picture and other types of trees are now harvested. Tourism has obviously flourished during this century; today, Algonquin offers the alternatives of the complete wilderness situation or the more traditional campground environment.

Ralph was born at West Guilford, Haliburton district some eighty years ago shortly after which his family moved to Kearney. He has spent a life-time in service and appreciation of the out-doors. Since the age of seventeen, he has been associated with the park in various roles. He was a guide for sixty continuous summers. He has been involved with tourist promotion, hunting and fishing lodges, and winter trapping. Moreover, his untold hours of work related to this field have been given on a voluntary basis.

Ralph has contributed to his district in other capacities. He was a council member in Kearney for twenty years, which included a seven-year stint as mayor and he also served as a school trustee for a few terms.

Ralph has trapped in the Park's western section for decades, along the way developing innovative trapping techniques which have resulted in the production of some of Canada's finest pelts. Moreover, he has made his accumulated knowledge available to others through the courses he has taught for the Province at Elliot Lake. Today he teaches one for Georgian College. He has written his weekly *Along the Trail* column since 1970 for the Almaguin News of Burk's Falls. His participation with children's camps and school classes is noteworthy. During his visits, it is not uncommon for him to bring wild animals along to enhance the discussion.

The Bice family is a large group whose affiliation with the Park spans six generations. Ralph tells me, for instance, that his grandfather was one of the first poachers to be arrested in the Park.

Today at 80, Ralph remains an active and vital member of his community. His participation in several organizations has been recognized with the presentation of many distinguished awards. His vast knowledge of this topic will be recorded through the publication of this book and an important part of our heritage will be documented. He has supplied several vintage photographs to illustrate his stories. In some cases, the archives' collection is not as extensive.

But to understand the essence of the man, one must read his own words. This book is filled with tales of a bygone era, as well as detailed information to satisfy the dedicated outdoorsman.

I extend my congratulations to Ralph on the completion of yet another successful project. To the reader I send best wishes, knowing that you will find this book thoroughly enjoyable.

Frank S. Miller

Treasurer of Ontario,
formerly Minister
of Natural Resources

Getting ready the weekly column.

Prologue

ALGONQUIN PARK is such a different place now. After all, more than two generations have gone since I first knew that Park. Today visitors drive there on a well-kept, well-paved highway, and expect to get into a motor boat when they go on the water. This I guess is now called progress, but so different than years ago when everyone went in on the train, when they went out on the water it was in a canoe or a row boat. However since that is the way the present generation wants things, I guess it has to be the way it will happen. *But such a change!*

Memories go back to the days when the cottagers paddled over to the headquarters for groceries, mail, or perhaps just to meet the train. So many canoes, and not even one motor boat. Other memories? The many evenings in the guides camp, listening to the older guides, and picking up useful information. The many dances both in the old guides camp and the Rec hall, or it might be paddling over to pick up Ex-Inspector Arthur Storie, and going to any one of a number of cottages for an evening of bridge. Even the many times I visited with rangers, both park and fire rangers, or just a pleasant chat with one of the many yearly visitors.

Then the years we had the camp on Eagle Lake, and our parties were the same people, year after year. Also that first supper, when it was expected, and rightly so, that it would be a meal of those finest of all lake trout. So many times I heard Steve Berthold remark, when every one had his fill, *'Well, that is what we came for.'* Then again it might be meeting parties away back in the woods, and spending a few minutes discussing the trails and fishing. Later when we had the camps at Rain Lake, the big parties, mostly family parties, and oh, such times we had. And after all the chores were finished, such especially pleasant evenings we had with the Pitt party. Then too those many nights with the Folsom party, sitting around the campfire at Eagle Lake. Also the later years at Rain Lake with that party of Insurance men, who came as much for a week of bridge as to catch fish.

But the real memories go back when you would be on a camping trip with a small party and really be away back, perhaps on a quiet river, maybe you had even worked your way into a new, or seldom visited lake. Everything was so quiet and peaceful! Possibly a camping spot where you could see both the sunrise and sunset. Then the evenings around the campfire, with only your own low voices, and the odd crackle of the fire and the night sounds. There would be special times sharing that finest of all 'sounds', silences between friends. I remember once when Mr. Folsom and I were alone on the Nipissing River and on one stretch with only the Pine-clad hills, and light breeze, we paddled for quite some time without either one saying a word. When we did get to a portage, or perhaps to pull the canoe over a beaver dam, I made the remark that we had not spoken for half an hour. His reply was that everything was so beautiful it would have been a shame to spoil it by talking. Then the next day you would be back on the more travelled routes, and there would be people, which would remind you that, for a while you not only enjoyed nature at its best, but also, for a while you had the feeling that you were a pulsating part of it. The memories of those isolated lakes, clean shore lines, the breezes, the sunshine and fresh air can never be forgotten.

Times I get to thinking about those old guides, rangers and fishermen, most of them long gone, and I get to wondering if those kind of people go to heaven. If they do, there is hardly any doubt that they would be disappointed, for there could be no place, absolutely no place that would be as soul satisfying and tranquilizing as was the finest camping and fishing area that the Almighty ever created. Speaking of creations, we read in GENESIS, CHAPTER ONE, VERSE 31, *(the sixth day)*, *God looked out upon the world and all that he had made, and saw that it was very good.* I am quite certain he was looking at that spot we now call ... ALGONQUIN PARK.

Preface

It seems as if I have known about ALGONQUIN PARK as long as I can remember, There were the twice a year trapping trips that my Dad made, and it was always so nice when he came home again. Then there would be the times that fur had been brought home in the green state, and the fur would have to be stretched and dried ... Those were memorable days. Just to sit and watch, and listen to my Dad, my uncles and my grandfather talking about trapping. They still had a sore spot about being forced to leave their trapping grounds when that area had been set aside and trapping and hunting prohibited. The Park had been established in 1893, and my memories go back to very early in this century. It took some time for a young man to understand that this then far away place called Algonquin Park would some day be part of my life.

Times I get to wondering what it could have meant if things had been done differently. The idea of setting aside such a large area might have been accepted better by the people that experienced some hurt ... The establishing of the Park was a fine idea, especially at that period. The area in spite of earlier reports was not suitable for farming. It contained the headwaters of several rivers, and did make an excellent fishing and holidaying area. I do know that some men who had trapping grounds there were paid to leave, at least their camps were bought, though I do not imagine much money changed hands. At Kearney, *Tim Holland had a hunting camp on Eagle (Butt) Lake, and his camp was purchased by the Department; in fact it was used as a shelter hut until Dan Ross built one on the north side of the lake a few years later. *Jim Sawyer had a camp on that same lake, and the walls can still be

---

*TIM HOLLAND, *one of Kearney's ealiest settlers and trapper*
*JIM SAWYER, *an Uncle of Ralph Bice and a trapper*

found, that date back to the mid-eighteen-seventies. He was just told to move. So many trappers had camps, and they just were told there would be no more trapping in that section of Ontario.

People kept on trapping even though it meant mostly nightwork. My grandfather's camp was on what is called Roseberry Lake, and records show that he was the first trapper apprehended in the new Park. He had just reached his camp the day before, and was wondering what was going to happen, when Dan Ross showed up and informed him that he could not trap there any more. He was not charged, just told to take his equipment and leave ... But even when there were many Rangers, trapping still continued. To me, there was always the wonder about that then far away place, on Roseberry Lake, and I knew some day I would have to see it.

In the Summer of 1910, my father and an uncle were asked to go to Algonquin Hotel at Joe Lake and act as guides for summer visitors. When Dad came home he had so many stories to tell. Then snapshots came in the mail, and more than ever I felt I had to see that enchanted spot. For one thing, I just could not believe that there would ever be a job where you went fishing every day, and into the bargain got paid for it. I think it was then that I decided some day I would be a guide, and rightly or wrongly I did get that chance in 1917, and never missed a summer after that ... The idea of living outdoors, on such nice lakes, and the then main work being fishing was what made me so anxious to get to Algonquin Park. Fishing away back then was done when there were no more chores to do. Getting the cows from the pasture, helping with the milking, then two miles to school and more chores when you got home. I never did quite understand why there were always gardens to hoe, also berries and potato bugs to pick, just when the fishing was best ... Only I did get plenty of fishing in the more than sixty years I guided and operated a small business in the Park ... I have seen a number of my friends go into business, or get employment with larger companies and now they are retired and driving around in nice cars while I still have a battered old pick-up. There have been times I almost got to wishing I had tried some other type of livelihood, if just to see what I might have been able to accomplish. Then I got to thinking about all the fine people I have been associated with, those wonderful canoe trips where I enjoyed the trip as much as the people paying the bill. Having all the fresh air and all the freedom, I realize that I am one of the few who have done what they wanted to do.

The Park has changed so, but then so has everything else. There are so few of us left who can recall the days during the First War. Naturally we would prefer things as they were in the olden days, but we would be a very small minority ... Then there are times I get to wondering what Dickson* and Kirkwood* would say if they saw the way their pet project was going ... But while the highway is busy, some of the lakes crowded, and the fishing far from what we remember, there are still many places where you can feel you are back in the woods. The loons and other birds sound just as nice, the breezes just the same, and the woods and the waters still give one that contented, peaceful feeling.

It was some time ago that I sort of planned on writing a story about Algonquin Park. The first title was to have been Forty Years in Algonquin Park, and now it could be changed to Seventy Years. It is not really a history and I did not have to look up a lot of early data, Audrey Saunders* has done that. So I am just jotting down what I remember about the different lakes and rivers and some interesting things that happened during those years. So few of the stories we read about the Park mention Rangers or Guides, so there will be a chapter on those people. I will no doubt miss some names of both guides and rangers, but since most are long gone, it may be a while before they can find fault with what I may write.

Most of what I have written is from my own experience, and some from things told me by my father, also a few from Grandad. Some dates may not be absolutely accurate, but not too far out. Just remember that guiding and trapping do not give one the training to do much writing, which is why I have tried to put this down just as if I was telling it around a campfire.

Hopefully, as a result of this book, my children, grandchildren and my great grandchildren, in fact all, who visit Algonquin Park, will experience a bit of the feeling I have for *the greatest of all outdoor playgrounds.*

---

*ALEXANDER KIRKWOOD *Chief Clerk in the Land Sales Division, Ontario Department of Crown Lands, and originator of the idea in 1885 of a 'National Forest and Park' in the Algonquin Highlands.*
*JAMES DICKSON *Ontario Land Surveyor, who first conducted surveys in the area of the proposed park in 1879, and recommended it for preservation.*
*AUDREY SAUNDERS *Author of Algonquin Story, 1963, Ont. Dept. of Lands and Forests.*

Ed Godin, one of the early forest rangers.

My First Trip
Into Algonquin Park

My first trip into Algonquin Park was in 1912. My father was a Ranger with a beat that took in the area that Butt, or as it was then called Eagle Lake, as the central spot. The Rangers had several cabins, or shelter huts as they were called, which meant that the men had accommodation when they travelled and patrolled their given areas.

As I recall it now, Father, and his partner R.J. White, better known as Bob, had besides their main camp at Eagle Lake, one at Roseberry Lake, and one which was shared by the Rangers from the north at Tims Lake.

I cannot recall if it was July or August, but it was when school was out. I was twelve years old at the time, and with a younger brother, was taken into the woods for a week. The journey from Kearney to Rainy Lake was an event in itself. We left Kearney at about nine in the morning, and journeyed sixteen miles to our point of embarkment.

I don't remember much about Rainy Lake. My brother (George) and I were too anxious to get into the canoe and get going. I do know that we went to the Shelter Hut which was the Headquarters of Dan Ross, one of the original four Park Rangers (see Algonquin Story, by Audrey Saunders), and his wife, some children and grandchildren were there for a holiday. The girls in the party were complaining about sleeping in tents when the nights were cool, but one thing I will never forget is the very heated argument Bob White and Dan Ross got into about the coming federal election. Anyone who was around then, 1912, will remember it was an election in which reciprocity was the issue. I could not understand why two men could have such definite ideas, when one of them had to be wrong. This was not my first object lesson in politics, that occurred four years previous when we lived on a so-called farm in Haliburton. After the federal election, my mother had cut the picture of Sir

Wilfrid Laurier out of the paper and hung it on the kitchen wall. He had led the Liberals to victory. I can still see the look my father gave it when he came in. It was some time before I had the courage to ask him why he burned it.

After lunch we got started on our trip. Bob White was to come in with a load of lumber for a new camp they were building, and we went on to the camp at Eagle Lake. There were portages, and on the second portage we met a party of campers. Dad knew the guides, and there was the usual discussion of fishing and weather. There were two ladies in the party, and they were washing the dishes in the lake. Later I read that eating utensils should be taken to the lake and scoured with sand, but like so many of the written rules of the woods, that system does a rather poor job.

It was late in the afternoon when we arrived at Eagle Lake, which I thought then and still think is just about the most beautiful lake, not only in Algonquin Park, but in Ontario. After getting out a few articles inside the camp, we walked to the previous party's campsite, One of the guides, Sam Hollingshead, had told Dad there were a few groceries there for him. There was coffee, and we had some for supper. The fragrance of coffee and balsam boughs as everyone knows is one of the best in the woods. This was my first experience with it, and one I have never forgotten.

The next day we moved on to Roseberry Lake, where the new cabin was to be built. We stayed in the old cabin, which was built near the spot where my Grandfather had his trapping camp, years before the area had been declared a Park. It is still a lovely spot, with a very fine sand beach all along the north side of the lake.

Roseberry Lake was called Round Lake by the early trappers, but the name was changed early in the history of the Park. It is not a large lake, also not a very deep lake. Years ago the fishing for both lake and speckled trout was excellent, but heavy fishing in such a small area of water has depleted the lake. There is still good fishing there at times but not what it was when I first saw it.

Records show that there was once an Indian camp on this lake. The water is a reddish colour, and it appears the Indians came to this lake for the red clay which they used as paint. The lake would be on the route between Georgian Bay and the Petawawa River. The trail came up the Magnetewan River as far as navigation would permit, over the height of the land to the head of the Pine River (now called the Tim River) and thence down stream to where it emptied into the Petewawa at White Trout Lake. Just how old the camping ground is had been a topic of discussion for years. Some of the arrowhead points and artifacts, when examined by experts, show that it is one of the very oldest camping grounds. The pieces that have been found show samples of stone from several sections of Ontario, which would go to prove that there was considerable trading being done, even a couple of thousand years ago.

At the time of our stay at Roseberry Lake, the Booth Lumber Company was building a dam at the foot of Long Lake (now called Longbow). Roseberry and Long came together near the outlet of Long and the dam built up quite a head of water. In fact it was raised so high it eventually flooded the new rangers cabin, destroyed a lot of trees and ruined the shore line of two very beautiful lakes. So-called lumberman's rights have spoiled a lot of shore line all over Algonquin Park.

I caught my first lake trout in Roseberry Lake. The tackle was what nearly all the natives used at that time, a hand line consisting of a line heavy enough to be a chalk line, and it had ever so many sinkers on it. I do not imagine the line went very deep, as the size of the line would create quite a resistance. With the lakes so full of fish as they were in those days it did not matter too much, but at the present time I rather imagine this method of fishing would produce very few fish. Too, such a line is quite hard to drag around when paddling.

But I did catch a trout, — several in fact. There was a doe with two fawns standing in the water, and when we were getting close to them the fish struck. I think I was more interested in the deer than the fish, and I forgot all about piling the line neatly. The resultant confusion made quite a mess of the line, and I think it took Dad some time to untangle it. The fish weighed I imagine about eight pounds. Since then I have caught many trout, and have been in charge of the canoe when much larger fish were taken, but that fish was the largest I myself have taken.

Being youngsters my brother and I asked many questions about the old trapping camp that had belonged to our Grandfather, and at that time there were a few logs of the wall still standing, as well as a lean-to shed. Dad told us that he had made his first trip into that camp when he was seventeen, which was in 1888. He did not come in to trap, but had been hired to shoot deer for a lumber camp, situated at the head of Long Lake. The deer had been fairly numerous for a few years, and the lumber company had hoped to get a good supply of meat. The pay was to be four cents per pound. All supplies had to be toted* in from Sundridge at that time, and anything that did not have to be toted in would be a big help. The snow records, while quite heavy for the two winters previous to that, were not excessive that winter. There were not too many wolves, but for some reason or other the deer had disappeared. Dad told us that he had hunted two days with a good pair of deer hounds, and had not got a start. He finally gave it up, and did a bit of trapping, as it was not worth while trying to hunt when there were no deer.

It may seem strange that hounds would be taken so far into the woods. At that period, when hunting with dogs, most of the deer were killed in the water. Good fast deer hounds would drive a deer into the water, and it was then easy to paddle up and shoot it in the head. Quite a saving on meat and ammunition. Since it was a three day trip from home to camp, it must have been quite a job to take two hounds in a canoe, and manage them on the portage.

We waited for the team and wagon to bring the lumber into Roseberry Lake. The road was in very good shape for a wagon. It had not been used for a number of years, but it went mostly on high ground and for that time it was considered a good tote toad. I remember that Dad spent two days repairing bridges, and finally on Friday we went back to Eagle Lake. I can still see my Dad's chagrin and perhaps a bit of anger when we found the lumber and supplies piled at David Lake. Seems like the team could only be had for two days, and then had to go back. This meant all the lumber, roofing etc. had to be carried over the portage from Pomberry to Roseberry, a measured distance of two and a quarter miles.

The shelter hut stood for many years. During the time that lumber operations were being carried on it was not possible to use it when the waters were in flood. During the summer it was a very handy place to drop in and stay when travelling. In the summer of 1921 my eldest brother and I were there with a party of fishermen. We arrived just before lunch, and while I was unloading packs and getting a fire started, he took two men out to catch fish for lunch. I do not think that more than fifteen minutes passed before he was back with two very nice fish, plenty for the five of us for lunch. When cleaning them at the shore he called to us to come see the fresh minnow in one fish. It was a perch, several inches long. He laid it back in the water, and it made a few weak movements, finally straightened up and swam away. Must have been swallowed only a few minutes before the fish was caught. Perhaps the story about Jonah was right after all.

Another event took place in Roseberry Lake years later. We were with a party of American fishermen and were camped on Tims Lake. We took a day trip to Roseberry, which is a few miles down stream from Tims. My father and also my oldest brother were guiding them. One of the fishermen caught a fine speckled trout perhaps four or four and a half pounds. When we cleaned it the stomach was distended, and anxious to see what the fish were eating, we looked. Inside was a small otter. This may seem strange, but there is no doubt what it was. The only answer, (it was in May), seems to be that someone was trapping on the lake, caught an otter — opened it and threw the not fully developed kit into the water. (This was recorded in Miss Saunder's book). Contrary to general belief, speckled trout are scavengers. It is not uncommon to be eating lunch on a rocky point and afterwards catch a speckled trout that had eaten everything that had been tossed into the lake, even the remains of cooked fish.

---

*Portaged over a bush trail

My First
Guiding Trip

It is over sixty years since I went on my first trip as a guide but I do not think I will ever forget it. I had been working for the Forestry Branch burning bush, and early in August was asked by Ed Colson* if I would go on a trip with a party of campers. He explained that the party was already in the woods, but one of the guides, Charley McCann, had to leave the party at Merchants Lake, and they needed a replacement. When I arrived at Joe Lake I found I had to take a pack of supplies, which meant I would have to make two trips on the portages. Since I had never been on any of the lakes or streams, I was just a little skeptical about making it to Merchants Lake that day. I did get as far as Minnessing Camp for lunch in spite of a heavy head wind and started up Island Lake as soon as I could.

I was using my own canoe, the first one I had owned. It was a board canoe, and there were many in use then (1917). They were easier to paddle than the wider canvas covered canoes, but were not as nice to carry.

I had a good map, and had no trouble finding my way through the Otterslides, and reached White Trout Lake late in the afternoon. The wind was still very strong, blowing quite hard, and there was a heavy swell piling right into the bay where the creek from Otterslides enters White Trout. It took quite a long tme to get across the lake, and the first bay I tried, looking for the way to Merchants, proved to be the wrong one. I finally found the right bay, but after paddling what seemed miles, there was still no sign of the portage. The sun had been long gone and I knew if I didn't locate the trail that I would not be able to find my way after dark. There were a few beaver dams that I had to pull the canoe over, and I was really beginning to think I might be off track, but just above one dam there was a freshly cut log which raised my hopes. I was more than a little tired, so I decided to stop for the night. Both sides of the creek were very marshy, and there was no sign of any high ground, so I just rolled into my blankets and went to sleep. The only thing that bothered me was the fact that I had had no supper, and no prospects of any until I found my party.

Several times during the night I heard wolves howl, and just at daybreak a deer jumped into the water only a few feet from the canoe. I was startled to say the least, even more so when it seemed like a tremendous sized pack of wolves started to howl right at the edge of the timber. I have since been told that no doubt the wolves halted when they became aware of my presence, and gave voice to their disappointment of being deprived of their breakfast. Several times since, I have been in similar situations, but that morning to a seventeen year old boy it sounded like all the wolves in the Park were headed my way.

I was only a few yards from the portage trail, and did not tarry on the trail over to Merchants. When I did get to the lake, I had no idea where my party was camped. From the centre of the lake there was finally a sign of people, and it was not long until I was devouring a belated breakfast. The guides were all from Huntsville. In charge was Angus McLennan, with whom I made several trips in later years. Fred May, one of the well-known guides half a century ago, and George Markle, who like myself was making his first trip as a guide.

The fishing in Merchants Lake at that time was fabulous. There were great quantities of lake trout, some of them getting to a real good size. For years it was not uncommon to hear of twenty-five or even a thirty pounder being caught. During the mid-twenties Charlie Skuce, fishing with a partner from Northway Lodge, caught one that when weighed two days later, went thirty-five pounds. I think that is the largest lake trout I know of that was caught by angling during the time I have been in the Park.

There was also a little lake quite close to Merchants called Chickadee Lake — also full of fish. It was only a step over to Green Lake, (now called Happy Isle), where there were also quantities of lake and speckled trout. These two lakes still produce a lot of fish.

There is another lake to the north of Green or Happy Isle Lake, Red Rock. This lake became very popular late in the twenties. When I started to guide there only a few people knew that it was full of speckled trout. Dick Blackwell, I believe, was the man who first fished in the lake, and for several years the matter was kept fairly secret. At that time, a very obscure trail went from Happy Isle a distance of nearly two miles. Later a trail was cut from Opeongo and again from Crow River. With the heavy influx of fishermen in that area over the last twenty years, I can easily imagine that Red Rock too has been heavily fished.

About a week after I joined Ed Colson's party of campers, we left for McDougall Lake, where the party wanted to do some bass fishing. This lake is now known as Booths Lake, but still produces many fine catches of bass. There is good lake trout fishing as well.

We broke camp early in the morning, and I was very interested in how quickly the tents were taken down, and all equipment packed. There was a lot of luggage, for we were to be in the woods another two weeks. Though there were four guides, we had to each make three trips on the portages. It had been our original plan to camp part the way down Opeongo but there was hardly any wind, and the older guides thought we should go right through in case it became windy the next day. The decision about the camp at Annies Dam was a good one, for the wind got up early the next day, and we would have had trouble with our very heavily loaded canoes on the larger part of the lake.

The fish hawks or ospreys, apparently had a nest not too far away, We saw them every day, and occasionally left small fish in the water not far away from shore. The first hawks that came for the fish were a bit on the scared side, but after a day or two they showed no fear, and we saw them dive for the fish many times.

The dams on both Opeongo and McDougall Lake were not in workable condition then. It was in the late thirties that Booths improved those two and other dams as well, in order to drive their logs to Barrys Bay. The dam on McDougall made for a much larger volume of water in the lake and also prevented the bass from going on down stream. At least it improved the bass fishing. I have not been there for many years, but recall that you could not have asked for better bass fishing. By reports it is still a good place to fish bass.

From this camp Fred May and I made a trip to Booths' Farm. This was a large clearing, not far from the river a short distance below McDougall Lake. This had been for the same purpose as other lumber camp farms, but had not been in use for a number of years. Well over a hundred acres of land had been cleared, but by the number of stones and rocks around I doubt if it produced much as a farm.

One large rock sat alone a ways out in the field, and Fred suggested that we go and see it. It was known as J.R. Booth's armchair. There was a depression in the stone, and it was quite comfortable to sit in,, and not hard to imagine you were in a chair. The rock was ten feet high, and a human felt small sitting in this so-called chair.

It was at the farm on this trip that I first met Mort Finlayson. He was one of the oldtimers in that section of the Park, and then and years afterwards, was a Fire Ranger. In subsequent trips I had several occasions to talk with him, and learned many of the stories about the early years in that section of Algonquin Park, as well as before it had been a Park.

He was one man who was supposed to have returned with the Dennison boy to the head of the Opeongo Lake when the boy's grandfather was fatally mauled by a bear caught in a trap. Later it was Finlayson who hunted and found a man who had been lost in the woods for twenty-three days. The man, whose name I have forgotten, was well up in years, but recovered and lived years longer, in spite of his ordeal.

We left McDougall Lake a day or two earlier than we had planned. There had been a couple of days of heavy rain, and the older guides, from past experience, figured that the water in the river would be as high as it would get before dropping again. There were no fast rapids but the high water made travelling easier.

We reached Crotch Lake about noon, and there for the first time I met one of the original Park Rangers. Eli Donjini was then well up in years and had been a Ranger since shortly after the Park was established. His partner was Jack Stringer, who ranged for years, and lived for many more years after that.

The pine trees were still there on my early visits to Crotch Lake. One of the first things that Fred May did was to take us all over to see what he called the twin pines. Two trees, quite large ones, stood about twelve or fifteen feet apart. Perhaps twenty feet from the ground a limb from one of the trees had made contact with the other tree, and continued to grow. The limb itself was at least a foot in diameter, and my first thought when I saw it was 'what a wonderful place for a swing'. No one ever came up with an explanation of how the limb became joined to two trees. There is a similar one on Butt Lake also with pine trees, but the distance is less than a foot. Eli told us that an old Indian had told him that it had been done as a joke by Indians when the trees were small. Nevertheless, it was an oddity, and perhaps should have been taken to a museum. When the log markers came along there was no sign of sentiment, and the trees went the way of all pines.

There were a lot of pine around Crotch Lake at that time. The J.R. Booth Lumber Company had a camp at Billies Lake, about two miles west from Crotch Lake, and had built a railroad in from the siding at Egan's Estate. The logs were taken by train to Ottawa.

On the East side of the lake was perhaps the finest stand of white pine that grew in that section. Indeed I doubt if there was a finer stand anywhere in Ontario. The trees were large, they grew on a level piece of land that sloped slightly upward from the lake, and the trees came right down to the waters edge. There were very few other trees, except an odd small balsam. The expression then was that you could drive a wagon in amongst the trees. There are no such forests of pine to see now. I was fortunate enough to have seen Crotch Lake before the pine was cut, and it was a most magnificent sight.

Many of the trees were more than three feet in diameter, and there did not seem to be any small ones. Too, it appeared that the trees were being cut at the peak of their growth, as there were very few culled logs to be seen in the areas that had been cut.

Miss Raymond and I made a trip to the lumber camp for a few needed supplies, as some of our stock was getting low. There was not much activity, as they were then getting ready for the fall cutting.

Next, Fred May and I were sent to Victoria Lake, a few miles downstream, to make arrangements for the horse and wagon to take us from Victoria Lake to Egan Estate.† I do not recall the name of the man who made the trips, but for several years this man transported camping parties to and from Victoria Lake to Egan Estate.

There was and still is a large private lodge on Victoria Lake. It was owned by a Senator Smith, who I believe came from Vermont. The caretaker was a man named Hamilton. For a number of years they exercised control over the fishing in Victoria Lake, but the next year, which would be 1918, parties complained of being ordered off the lake, and it was later found that it was not a private lake, and the fishing was for the public.

There was a large family of Hamiltons, and later I guided with some of the boys. I have been told that the present caretaker is also named Hamilton, a grandson of the man who was in charge when I first visited the lake.

Senator Smith owned a large parcel of land which encircled the lake. The ownership changed a few years ago, following the death of Mr. Smith.

There was another quite large camp where the road came to the lake, and it was called Chamberlain Lodge. I was told that he had had some connection with the railroad, but for the few years that I was near there I never saw it occupied.

We did not stop at Victoria Lake, but met the horses and wagon at the landing. The trip out to the railroad was uneventful, and we caught the afternoon train and returned to the hotel that afternoon.

I made another trip three weeks later, also with Angus McLennan and Fred May, and travelled the same route as on my first trip. Among my most treasured memories is the thrill that occurred when first I saw the Crotch Lake pine stand, perhaps the most impressive sight in Ontario at the time.

Early Park Ranger, operator of Highland Inn and Algonquin Hotel.
†*Property of John Egan, Irish Immigrant, who became a leader in Ottawa Valley Logging. Egan Timber Limits on the Madawaska came into the hands of J.R. Booth, after Egan went bankrupt and died.*

The Long Drive

In almost all of the stories about Algonquin Park, mention is made of the famous and unusual log drive when the Gilmore Lumber Company drove pine logs all the way from their limits in the Park to their sawmill at Trenton. The operation was a costly one, but the length of the drive, meaning the distance from the standing timber to the sawmill, made it the topic of conversation for many years when the subject of log drives was mentioned.

This could not be considered the greatest distance logs have been taken by water to a mill. Just about that same time, an American company had cutting rights to a tract of timber in Butt Township in Nipissing District. These logs, many of them large ones, were driven all the way down the Magnetewan River to Byng Inlet, then boomed and towed to Bay City, Michigan. I saw a record where it stated that on one of the drives the logs averaged just over five hundred board feet per log. Even with the log rule used in those days, it meant for quite large logs.

What did make the *Gilmore drive* unusual was that logs were taken on three different waterways. Since company headquarters was at Canoe Lake and the camps were in that area, it meant that the first river used was the Oxtongue. Next would come the Black River, and finally the Gull River waters for the rest of the trip to Trenton.

My father worked in one of the camps the first winter, in fact, the first two winters. The camp he was in was built right beside where the dam is at the foot of Joe Lake. Gilmore's had a reserve dam there when they were cutting logs, and it was still standing when I was there first in 1914. At that time, too, the foundations of the old camps were easily distinguished, as they had not all rotted away.

I should have mentioned the great numbers of pine trees in the area. When

I was first there, fires had burned away the slash, and the new growth had not hidden the stumps. What a pine forest it must have been! Dad had told us several times, that in the two winters he worked there they did not get far enough from the camp to make it necessary to carry a lunch. Too, I have been told that this was one of the first operations where they did not use oxen, only horses.

For quite a few years after I began to work in the Park, the old camps were still standing. I believe there were eleven camps in all, and these were grouped in an area that now would be handled by perhaps only one. But apparently the men in charge wanted plenty of logs, so plenty of camps.

The foreman in the camp where Dad worked was Con O'Donnell, who later lived in Kearney. I went to school with his children. I do not believe he followed the drive, though his brother, Martin O'Donnell, was one of the men in charge.

My father could not recall the names of all the foremen at the different camps. Besides Con O'Donnell, he remembered Joe and Hugh McCormick, John Hicky, Joe Cox, Jim Chambers, Ed Casijean, and Sam Gunther, a son of the Walking Boss,* P.M. Gunther. He did not say for certain that Ed Cassidy was a camp foreman, but he was head man in charge of the drive. Many people will still remember Ed Cassidy. He had a service station just north or east of the swing bridge in Huntsville, and for a number of years was a fur buyer.

Logs were cut in the woods much later in the spring than is now done. No doubt because of the short haul to water. Many of the men stayed in camp after cutting finished, as it was a long way home, and the drive would start as soon as weather and ice permitted. A thaw did come fairly early, but cold weather returned, and it looked like the spring flood would get away before the lakes were clear of ice. So, as a matter of necessity, the ice on Potter Lake was dynamited so the logs could get started on their long journey. The date Dad gave me was April 28th, but I am not certain if this is the date of the blasting of the ice or the date the logs started to move. Whichever it was, the water would still be cold, and since the creek from Potter Lake to Canoe Lake was too small for a boat, it would mean a lot of wading.

At Canoe Lake the drive merged with the logs coming down from Joe Lake, and at Tea Lake with the logs from Smoke Lake. The rest of the drive to Lake of Bays and Dorset was uneventful.

A mile south of Dorset the lumber company had built an endless chain, something in the same style as the jack ladder used on many mills to lift logs from the water into the mill. From the top of the hill the logs went in a trough for a mile, and then an endless chain put the logs into Raven Lake, then Black River, and on into Hollow Lake. Hollow Lake was dammed to raise the water higher, and a trench dug in one of the lower spots so water and logs could go through a swamp to Harvey's Marsh, and a canal dug from there to St. Norah's Lake. The rest of the way was, as I said, all Gull River waters. The drive only got as far as Healy Falls, near Campellford, and stopped on October 1st.

Dad also worked in the camps on the drive the second year, but while they had the experience of the first year to help,water was low and the drive stopped on October 13th at Lakefield. This was a bad year, as they had a heavy fall of snow, twenty-two inches, at Fenelon Falls, early in October, and the men often worked in frozen clothes.

One thing Dad mentioned was that there was good food, and plenty of it. For most of the way, the cook camp must have been on top of a raft or crib. The highest wages paid were $28.00 per month, which included board.

Apparently there was a third cut, and a third drive, in which my father did not take part, and this drive did make Rice Lake the same year. But in the three drives, no logs reached the mill the first year.

Just about that time, the Canada Atlantic Railroad was built by J.R. Booth†, the famous lumberman, Gilmore's built a sawmill at Canoe Lake, but this, too, was costly, as it was over a mile from the railroad, and a long siding had to be built. Then it was discovered that the quality of the pine was not good. Rot had begun to show in most of the trees, and that meant low-grade lumber. With heavy operating costs, returns did not allow for producing low-grade lumber, and operations ceased early in this century.

When I first worked in the Park in 1914 there was still a lot of talk about the wasted pine lumber, and how three-inch boards, called *deal*, had been used to fill in wet places in order to pile lumber.

It's hard to understand why the pine would be of such poor quality. The Huntsville Lumber Company also used Canoe Lake as headquarters for just a few years later, and the logs they cut were driven to Huntsville. Much of the timber, instead of being poor quality, was used for square timber, and such timbers would only be accepted if they were number one pine.

About that time, the first lumbermen were cutting pine in Proudfoot Township, and I have been told that the pine those early cutters took was about the finest that was found anywhere in Ontario.

I worked along the railroad east of Canoe Lake in the summer of 1914. There is a creek, not too large, that follows the R.R., or perhaps the R.R. followed the creek. The creek rises in a few marshy ponds, perhaps two or three miles from Canoe Lake. This creek had been improved, no doubt for a log drive, all with sluiceways. No one could tell me anything about any drive on that creek, but it looked like the lumbermen in those days did not like to haul logs any distance if they could be transported by water.

Just a bit of humour in all this. On the first drive, my Dad, who was twenty-one at the time, and some of his buddies around the same age discovered an apple orchard, and since it was just about picking time they decided they should have some. Only thing, before they had really got started they met the owner, who gave them quite a lecture about stealing apples, and I believe even complained to the foreman. I never was told if there was a penalty.

Years later, my father met a school teacher, and they were married. You can imagine my father's surprise and perhaps embarrassment when he went to claim his bride at her father's home, to find that his future father-in-law was the same man who had given him such a hard time when he was caught stealing apples.

The dates and names concerning the drive I got from my father a few years before he died. Perhaps if I had thought of it years ago, I might have obtained more information. But it was quite an adventure, going in from Dorset, no doubt staying at the half-way house at Hardwood Lake (walking) and next day making camp. All winter with only the same crew, balsam bush bed, working ten hours a day, six days a week. Guess they made a tougher breed of men then. But in all the drives and other operations in the woods, *the Gilmore drive* will have to be just about the most unusual in the history of logging.

A Superintendent or Foreman of several camps. Sometimes called 'Bull of the Woods.'
†*J.R. Booth — Lumber Baron, who at one time had over 4,000 shantymen in his employ and owned the largest railway ever built by one man. Booth died in 1925 at the age of 99.*

Early Trapping

This chapter has a special place among my memories, for I learned a lot listening to my grandfather many years ago.

The traveller in the woods today, in areas outside the Park, as well as inside, can see beaver or signs of beaver almost anywhere. This, in spite of the fact that they are being heavily trapped in all adjacent areas, as well as in some parts of the Park. It was not always like this. When the Park was established, the beaver were very scarce. Trappers of that era have told me that there were only a few known spots where there were families of beaver.

Many years ago fur sales were held every fall at Minden, on November the fifth. Most of the trapping was done then when the trappers could use a canoe, and that of course meant most of the fur was caught in October. With the great emphasis that today is put on prime furs, it would be interesting to see what a whole bundle of fur would look like if it was all caught in warm weather. Talking to some of the older trappers long since gone, they admit that the fur was a bit on the black side, but the buyers paid a fair price for it. I sometimes wonder what excuses the buyers used then to get fur at a low price.

In the year 1892, at the Minden fur sale, my father was the only trapper who had more than two beavers. He had caught four, all from one family or house. He was trapping that fall on the east side of White Trout Lake.

Years ago, when there was a closed season on beaver, it was often stated that the reason for the decline of the beaver population was over-trapping. It is possible that the trapping helped keep them down, but I think it is generally agreed now that there must have been a disease, which reduced their population almost to the point of extinction. In recent years there have been areas where beaver died off, and it is quite likely that is what happened to beaver years ago. In areas that are very heavily trapped, they seem to be increasing. About the time trappers were allowed to take some beaver, they were guarded as if they were something very precious. Now, in some places, they are considered to be a nuisance.

The people who chose the beaver as our National Emblem made a wise choice. A very prominent writer a few years ago claimed it was not the proper animal, as it was shy and lived in the mud. There is no wild animal however, that has contributed more to the Canadian ecomomy than the beaver. It has shown that it can survive and increase under the most adverse conditions, and the beaver is one of the few, if not the only, well-known animal that is found in all ten provinces. It was the beaver that sent the explorers looking for new trapping grounds, and for many years it was the standard of trade when furs were bartered for supplies with the early traders.

I do not know how many beaver there are in Algonquin Park. However, I do know that it makes for much better travelling on the small streams where there are beaver dams to raise the water. A great many park beavers were live-trapped, and areas where beaver were non-existent, have been re-populated with beaver caught in Algonquin.

In the days of which I speak, most of the fur was what is known as small fur. There were plenty of mink, marten and fisher, plus a few otter. I do not recall if I was ever told of the number of otter that trappers would bring home, but I heard several times about the ninety-two mink that Jim Sawyer caught one fall. He was trapping from his camp on Big Misty Lake. His line was from there over to the Pine River , upstream to the High Falls, over to Eagle or Butt Lake, where he had another camp, south from there to Daisy or Dividing Lake as it was then called, and down the Petawawa to Misty. Since trapping in those days was just a spring and fall affair, and the trips lasted only a month or a few days longer, the real trapping was not much over three weeks, which means that Sawyer caught four or five mink each day.

Marten were plentiful then, but the best marten catch I could find was one of sixty-seven, caught between Long Lake (now Longbow) and the Nipissing River. This also was a one man take, about the same time Sawyer caught his mink. In those days a catch of forty was not uncommon for marten.

Fisher appear to have been just about as numerous then as they are now. Like all wild creatures, these animals are more abundant some years than others, and where deer and wolves are plentiful, there will always be fisher.

Ralph Bice.

Isaac Bice, grandfather of the author.
Had camp on Roseberry Lake in 1871.

Will Boice, uncle of the author, early
trapper and the last one of the family
who built bark canoes.

Wes Bice, uncle of the author (*note the letters L.E.M. on canoe*). This was on all canoes, paddles, etc. used at Algonquin Hotel, built in 1907 and first operated by L.E. Merrill.

Dr. J.C. Devitt with Fred Bice. Happy Isle, 1933.

Ralph with wife Edna and their children.

Fish again — the 9th meal in a row. Mealtime in camp.

Ralph in 1921.

Ralph guiding Mrs. Joe Clarke,
Lake Louise, 1921.

Ed and Molly Colson, two of the
early people who helped make
Algonquin Park popular.

Dr. Keith Reynolds and Hon. Frank
Miller with Ralph Bice, when Ralph was
officially honoured by the
Government of Ontario.

Ralph out on the trapline with sleigh dog, Max.

The 1917 Deer Hunt

There were a lot of deer in Algonquin Park in the summer of 1917. I doubt if they were ever more plentiful anywhere, and it is almost certain they will never be again. Their abundance was caused by the great area that had been burned a few years previous, creating many acres of fresh food. Travelling on marshy streams, or near marshes on lakes, deer could be seen in number any time of the day. Knowledge of deer and their feeding habits were not so well-known then as now, but the deer did get extremely plentiful, in spite of the great many wolves that were also present.

There was a war, as we all know, and some official decided it would be a good idea to kill off some of the deer to help out the meat supply. The wisdom of this move has often been questioned, but the fact remains there were too many deer, and it was desirable to thin them out a bit. The hunting was done mostly along the railroad, as there was no other access to the Park then. Deer were shipped to Toronto each week, and the hunt lasted from early in November until well after Christmas.

I think there are only two of us left who took part. I was hired to hunt with my Dad, and we hunted at Brule Lake. The other remaining hunter is Jack Gervais, a retired Park Ranger, who at that time worked for the Grand Trunk Railroad, at the Highland Inn, in Algonquin Park. During the hunt everyone who lived in the area was permitted to participate and rifles and ammunition were supplied. I do not know if there was a record kept of the number shot but I think it was just under a thousand deer. The top marksman honour was won by Jack Gervais, who killed over a 100 deer. His hunting area was done in the vicinity of the Headquarters, where several other hunters were also operating.

There are several things worthy of note which came out of the hunt. One was that the deer were showing signs of inbreeding. By that I mean they were beginning to be smaller. Biologists may not agree with me, few of them ever do, (and vice versa), but in all the deer that were killed, and there were many splendid bucks, we did not take a deer that weighed 200 pounds. In the well-hunted areas at that time, deer of 225 and even 250 pounds were not uncommon, and few hunting groups returned without at least one that weighed over the accepted *big* size of 200 pounds. This may be only a coincidence, but with the records that show deer in other areas getting much smaller after years of inbreeding, I think it is only natural to assume the same trend might have been happening to the very heavy deer population in the Park at that time.

There were some very fine sets of antlers amongst the deer shot, one I think was perhaps the nicest head I have ever seen. I got this deer myself, while hunting alone, and was very proud of it. It was close to two hundred pounds. The antlers measured twenty-two inches between the tips, and there were ten points, besides the tips, on each antler.

Some very large does were accounted for. The largest was bagged by William Marshall, a Ranger, who also hunted near Brule Lake. His doe weighed 168 pounds, bigger than many of the bucks that were taken.

Persons who complain about the large number of wolves in Algonquin Park today should have been around in 1917. They were not so plentiful near the railroad, but later when we moved further in to hunt near McIntosh and Wolf (now Timberwolf), we found that there were wolves everywhere. The packs were not large, as they ranged from singles to groups of five or six, but they were everywhere. If you sat on the shore of either of the two lakes, or Misty Lake, for an hour, you would see singles and packs of wolves. None came very close, but there seemed to be so many of them.

As we were leaving to go home for Christmas, Dad planned on going to Eagle Lake to set out poisoned baits, which was the accepted way to take wolves then. It was mild and wet the day we walked from Misty to Eagle. We spent a day at Eagle, killed a couple of deer for wolf bait, and the next morning left for the railroad, as we would catch the train at McCraney for the short ride to Kearney. It had turned cold in the night and created a crust which often happens and then a light snow fell on the crust. We followed the summer portages and it was perhaps seven miles from the camp on Eagle Lake to the railroad. The snow fell after midnight, so it was fresh. This may sound like a lot, but on that walk we saw tracks of fifty-two wolves. As usual there were singles, doubles and groups up to seven. There may have been repeats, but it still proves there was a very heavy wolf population in the Park at that time.

Now this spoils the idea that wolves slaughter great numbers of deer as some of the wolf-haters think. It does not seem that the deer could have gotten as plentiful as they did. The fact remains that when we had our heaviest deer population, we also had our heaviest wolf population. If the wolves killed so many deer, how could the deer have increased to the numbers that were very much in evidence in the period that ended with the heavy winter of 1922-23?

There were several *incidents* worthy of recalling. Mark Robinson killed a large buck that dropped in its tracks. When he cleaned it there was no evidence of blood or a bullet hole. Closer examination showed the bullet hit one of the antlers close to the skull, and had splintered the bone right into the brain, killing it instantly.

One day while hunting near Misty Lake, I was sent to watch a certain ridge while Dad chased through a swamp. Perhaps because of the noise I made going through the woods, or perhaps the deer heard us talking, but just as I got to my post I looked toward the thick timber and there was a large deer standing, perhaps seventy-five yards away, almost in perfect range. I fired three shots before the deer moved, then it took a few steps and dropped. I could not understand how I had missed with the first two shots, but when we went to clean it we found that every shot had scored, each one well enough to have made a kill.

Another day we were hunting between McIntosh and Wolf Lake. It was my turn to chase, and I raised up two nice deer, both headed in the right direction. After the shooting I followed through, and when close enough called and asked about the luck. There had been a few shots and I was told Dad had two deer down. He told me where one was, and I attended to the necesary throat-cutting. When I got close he said the other deer was just there in a little hollow. He put down his rifle and went over to the deer, a large buck. Just as he grasped it by the antler to turn it over, it raised up, reached out with a front foot and with one motion slapped Dad across the shoulders and knocked him into the snow. It happened too fast to think much, and as the deer lunged at Dad, I just pointed my rifle and fired, luckily hitting the animal in the neck. The deer fell right onto Dad, and if the shot had missed there is no doubt Dad would have been injured.

There was a lot of discussion, pro and con about the hunt, the following summer. Many claimed it was a shame to shoot so many deer, but the others pointed out that in the areas where the kill had been the heaviest, there seemed to be as many deer as ever. It was also claimed that the quantity of meat supplied was negligible, as the meat went so rapidly it was hardly possible to purchase any. On the other side the cost was low, as it was an experiment.

A few years later, we had a very heavy winter, and there were accounts of deer dying on their feet. These had been chased into deep snow, and did not have the energy to get back to the trails. In summer there were very heavy fires further north, and many of our deer moved to fresh feed that always follows fires. With the result that by 1925 the deer population had started to decrease noticeably, and many blamed it on the deer killing in Algonquin Park (1917).

Whatever caused it, whether migration, disease, winter kill or lack of feed, the fact remains that deer were very scarce in Algonquin Park in the late

1920's. Deer were also scarce in the areas just outside the Park, so bad in fact sections that had been heavily hunted saw very few huntcamps occupied. I never heard the excuse offered by the people who blamed the scarcity of deer on the wolves, when the deer made their comeback in the 1940's.

Brushgang

It was in 1914 when I first saw Cache Lake. The First World War had just started. There had been many fires started by sparks and cinders from the engines of the trains that ran through Algonquin Park at that time. Many were indeed large fires. One that started at Brule Lake burned a large area all the way to Opeongo. Someone had come up with the idea that it might be a good idea to clean the brush and dead wood from close to the tracks, back far enough that cinders would not be so liable to light on inflammable material. There were not so many departments in Lands and Forests then, and the work was under the supervision of Mr. G.W. Bartlett, who was superintendent at that time. The foreman was Alex Watson, one of the Park Rangers, who had been a woods foreman in lumber camps. Since my father was a Park Ranger, he asked if I could be given a job. (My chum was an Englishman with whom I had worked that previous spring. He later returned to England, and was killed at Pashendale).

We arrived at Algonquin Park late that night, but found our way to the camp, which was just tents, and stretched on a side of a hill just across the bay from Highland Inn. And it was raining. Next morning we met the rest of the gang, not many men. Mrs. Watson was the cook, and a good one too.

The first morning was spent in 'Hanging Axes', and in the afternoon we went about a mile east of the station and started to clear brush. The work, as we went along, never did get interesting. The life of living in a tent, working with pleasant company, plus the good food made it easier to take, as well as the fact that there was very little work, and our wages of $1.00 per day seemed big to a fourteen year old boy.

After a stay at that location we moved to Source Lake. Since there was a road leading to Camp Nominigan, the moving was done with a wagon. After that we moved on the train or I should say the wayfreight. This was a more pleasant camp than the first one. We did some fishing in Source Lake, but caught very little. There was a timber slide on the creek, the remains of which might still show. There were two other boys in the gang, and we tried to catch fish in the pools. One thing I remember. was the number of large eels that had worked out onto the slide, and then run out of water and died. Some were well over three feet long.

Another thing I will not forget. Being young and perhaps careless, I walked out on an unsafe portion of the slide, and went through, not badly hurt, but the fish hook managed to imbed itself in my finger. I still can see the look on Bert Porter's face, as he used his razor to cut it out.

We finished the season at the old railroad camp at Sims Pitt. It was nice to get under a roof when the rains got cold in the fall and it was later in October when the work was called to a halt.

The next spring we again used the camps at Sims Pit. For the first part we burned brush that had been piled the previous year, but when the woods started to dry up we went back to cutting again.

Out first camp was again on Source Lake, but on the western end. We were there quite a while and since it was early we caught many fish along the shore. We had almost a new gang the second year, as only two or three of us repeated from 1914.

From Source Lake we moved to Brule Lake, and put up our camp about half a mile west of the station. This was a lovely location, as we had good water, and lots of room. One thing I do not recall, and that is how we put up with the flies and mosquitoes. There were no screens on the tents, and of course, none of the bombs and repellents that are to be found everywhere today.

A rather funny thing happened at this camp. I was working with the teamster, helping him with the chain, and other jobs. Once we had to find a trail for the horses around an old camp that no doubt had been used by men working on the construction of the Railroad. There were many bottles, which I was told to just pitch well out of the way, in case a horse should step on one. I was quite surprised to find one that was full, and on examination, saw that the seal had not been broken. Some of the older men were called, and it was decided to send for Tom Cope, who was supposed to be the best judge of whiskey in the gang. If experience and quantity produces taste judges, there is not a doubt he would qualify. He pronounced it drinkable, and that night the one bottle was shared by ten men. The boys and younger men were not allowed to touch it. No one ever knew the brand, all that was on the bottle was the word 'Millano', but the ten men were all fairly well oiled that evening.

At Source Lake Camp the first year, we found some stone ovens that the workmen, mostly Italians I think, had used to bake bread when building the railroad. On a hill, we found perhaps the best ones, simple conical ovens or hives. Fires were built inside, then drawn out, and the bread and everything else baked there. We had a couple of Europeans who had used similar ovens in the old country, and they explained how the ovens worked.

This memory was just stored away in my mind, and I do not remember ever thinking about them until a few winters ago. Then I saw that famous cook, Madame Benoit, on television, and she was explaining how these ovens were used. Then I remembered the Source Lake ovens. I passed along what I recalled of their location to the Park Superintendent, and using my directions, he walked right to them. Of course, they had fallen in.

The Women Who Helped Mould Algonquin Park

It seems fitting that some mention should be made of the women who were important to Algonquin Park years ago. Important at a time when it was still considered a man's world. So few have been remembered, yet all I will mention should have a high standing in the Algonquin Park hall of fame, that is if we had one. These women all contributed their share, or maybe more, when Algonquin Park was then considered back in the woods.

The first woman that comes to mind is one that I never saw. This would be Suzanne DuFond, wife of LaAmable DuFond, an Indian who had taken up land on the northern end of Manitou Lake. He had obtained a deed well before the Park was established, and was there until after World War One.

According to Peter Ranger, Suzanne DuFond, the first woman known to have lived in Algonquin Park, was a marvelous woodsman, or guess now I should say woodsperson, and could tell campers and fishermen just where the best fishing could be found.

Next, Molly Cox (Mrs. Ed. Colson), a nurse who came to Park Headquarters in the early days of this century. She came with a family, and liked it so well she remained as cook at the Ranger's boarding house. This was just about the time people began discovering the wonderful fishing in Algonquin Park.

Molly later married Ranger Ed Colson, and aware of the needs of summer guests, they had a tent camp set up. Then the Grand Trunk Railway built the Park's first hotel, and the Colsons were asked to take charge.

Molly was known as a careful manager, and took good care of her staff, and many times went out of her way to help people. It soon became known that she was a nurse, and since doctors were scarce, took over many times at sick beds. Just before the First World War the Colsons left, but returned in 1917 when they purchased Algonquin Hotel.

There are many stories still being told about the way Molly had helped people. Early in the spring of 1918, just after the ice was gone, there came a terrible storm. Two guides who worked from the hotel, Larry Dixon and George Rowe, had been visiting at Canoe Lake, a paddle of over a mile. Coming back in the rain and wind, a twister caught them, and their canoe was overturned. Worst of all, the force threw Larry Dixon against an upturned root, causing serious damage. Rowe managed to keep both of them above water, with the aid of old roots and logs, and called for help which he did not expect.

The Colsons were in bed, but heard the calls. They got dressed, got into a canoe, and found the two men, pretty far gone, but they got them back to the hotel. George Rowe was cold and wet, but the next day none the worse for his ducking. But Larry Dixon had internal injuries, and Mrs. Colson knew he had to get medical aid. So he went off to Toronto on the early train. My mother happened to be going to Toronto on the same train, and helped Mrs. Colson, who had been up all the previous night. Unfortunately, Dixon did not survive the operation.

The other incident was some years later, at the home of a family by the name of Farley, who lived near where the saw mill was located. A baby was expected and as these things happen, it came a bit ahead of time. No roads, the trains ran only twice each week, snow and ice, late in April, and the gas car could not make it. So, as per usual, send for Molly Colson. Molly had not been too well, and needed a cane to get around, but didn't hesitate to help. She walked more than a mile to the Farley house using two canes and all alone delivered a fine baby girl, who today works in a bank in Huntsville.

Perhaps I am a bit prejudiced, but one of my nicest memories will have to be the way Molly took care of the younger guides. There were a few of us not too old, and our own mothers could not have been more interested in the way we were treated. Not only the young guides, but all young peope were or seemed to be her special care.

Then we must mention Annie Colson. Sister to Ed, who had been in charge of the outfitting store at Highland Inn, and continued in that capacity when they moved to the Algonquin Hotel. She could set up a list of supplies as well as most guides, and a lot of people had better holidays because of this woman being there to give advice.

Another name that comes to mind is Mrs. Shannon Fraser. During the First World War, they had set up the old Huntsville Lumber Company boarding house as a small tourist camp. The main reason for its success was the reputation Mrs. Fraser had for putting up such wonderful meals. She had a daughter Mildred (later Mrs. Art Briggs), and sometimes other help, but the cooking was her special gift.

Among my summer memories, I recall the small twin daughters of Mark Robinson. I was treated more like an older brother by these girls. In fact we finally comprised a criminal ring, they were the purveyors and I the receiver. But since the goods were cookies from their Mother's jar, I can assure you that the evidence very quickly disappeared. Several times as I stood talking to Mark, I would feel a little hand near mine, and a cookie would change hands. So often, and this more than sixty years ago, I think of those two sweet little girls, who liked a guide well enough to rob the cookie jar for him.

Then there was Winnifred Traynor. Her father had been a camp foreman for the Huntsville Lumber Company, and lived at Canoe Lake. She was the lady, so much in the news, whenever stories were written about the artist Tom Thomson, who was drowned in Canoe Lake in 1917. In spite of the report of the undertaker, she always maintained that there had been foul play. When she died, she willed the cottage to her favourite nephew, who still summers there.

There is one woman I think should be mentioned. I do not know what her name was when I first met her, but she acted as a guide, even to outfitting her own parties. Several times she would be camped on Butt Lake, always on the island the same time as I was there, and we became pretty good friends. As far as I know, she was the only woman who acted as a guide in the Park. She was a small woman, but could carry a canoe, as well as her share of packs.

I had not seen her for many seasons, when a few years back she visited the Park with her husband and children. Her married name is Mrs. Kaiser.

The first years I was at Cache Lake, we often saw canoe loads of girls on camping trips. They were from Northway Lodge, the first girls camp in Algonquin Park. The camp had been started by Miss Fanny Case, and it was to this camp that Charley and Eddie Skuce came to guide, just after World War One.

Next was Miss Mary Hamilton. She built Tanamakoon Camp in White Lake, and from the beginning it was a success. She was fortunate to be able to have George May who was in charge of everything outdoors. She employed then, and for many years, licensed guides, and many times those of us who guided were glad to get a trip or two from this camp. Such a difference. On other trips when it became lunch time, the guides got the meal, cleaned up, and then travelled again. On these trips all there was to do, and not always that, was get some wood, sit down and be waited on.

Many boys and girls have spent enjoyable summers in Algonquin Park and a lot of the credit must go to the Taylor Statton Camps. The camp lore acquired on Canoe Lake and the nearby islands, provides outdoor education to thousands, a tribute to the good management of Mrs. Taylor Statton.

I believe all the ladies I have mentioned are gone, with the exception of Mrs. Kaiser and of course the twins. Together, these women and others helped to make the Park what it is today.

Algonquin Hotel

I am not just certain when the Algonquin Hotel was built. I imagine there must be records, but no one I have talked to seems to know. From what I can gather, it was built a year or two after the first Highland Inn was put up. Which suggests the Algonquin Hotel, located at Joe Lake, was built then in 1907 or 1908 by a Mr. L.E. Merrill. He operated the hotel until it was purchased by Mr. Ed Colson in the spring of 1917.

The Hotel was built well back from the railroad, on a hill, with a view looking out over Joe Lake. The outside was of slabs, especially cut for this building. It was well laid out and furnished, but I do believe that the same old furniture was there when it was torn down. I think the capacity was about thirty-five guests.

There was a train station, opened only in the summer months, built of cedar logs, and with a good fireplace. This was the property of the Grand Trunk Railway System.

The outfitting and grocery store was near the station, also the wharf. This was perhaps, during the banner years, the best outfitting store in Algonquin Park. That would be because Ed Colson was fully aware of what was necessary on a camping trip. Also, this store was presided over by Ed Colson's sister, and she was about the best person to ask advice from on what to take on a camping trip. She was known as Aunt Annie to all of the young people, and as she was around for many years, some who were not so young, still called her Aunt Annie, and were glad of her advice when getting an outfit together.

The first time I saw the Algonquin Hotel was in 1914. We were on the brush gang then, and camped at Sims Pit, and often passed it on the way to work. Too, we spent several evenings there with the caretaker and his family, late in the season.

Guides

Years ago when the greatest attraction the Park had for summer visitors was fishing, it was easily understood that a great many guides were needed. Not so many people knew much about canoeing, especially in the woods and besides, they were hardly qualified to make trips into unknown wilderness. So there were guides. In fact, they were almost as necessary as the canoes they paddled and carried. There were guides who took fishing parties into lakes that became part of the Park, some time before the Park was established. These men were able woodsmen, who needed to know how to set up a camp, prepare meals, find the better fishing, and most of all to be able to get along with people. There might be different personalities on each separate party. One thing, perhaps it was the idea that back in the woods distinctions ended, and most parties, in fact nearly all of them, came to enjoy their holiday.

As in all occupations and professions, some became more adept than others. Even at that, there were often times that the so-called second-raters came in with larger fish and a well-satisfied party. The top guides often had the same parties year after year. If the party was large and required two or perhaps several guides, the supposedly best guide was rated as head guide.

It is quite understandable that young guides or beginners would try and learn as much as they could from the more experienced. They found out that they could learn as much or more by just watching, rather than by asking questions, for like many other trades or occupations, people just do things, and it is sometimes hard to explain how it is done to others.

The disappearance of the guides was gradual. There was a magazine article in an American magazine called, *The Passing of the Guide*. The story was based on observations in the State of Maine, but everything in that article could have applied to Algonquin Park.

The first guide I really had much to do with was Ezra Ward. He was not guiding at the time, in fact I do not think he guided after that. We were working together on a gang, burning brush, and he did show me a lot about fishing, mostly for lake trout, as we had long evenings. Also, more than a few tips about setting up tents and getting along with different people. So when I left in early August that summer to go on a guiding trip from the Algonquin Hotel, I had acquired quite a few pointers.

I was very fortunate to be on a trip with two of the best guides in the Park. There were four guides, and the head guide was Angus McLennan of Huntsville. As well, there was Fred May, who at that time was considered the best outdoor cook in the Park. From these two I learned many tips that helped a lot in later years. I had two trips with those two, both on the same route. White Trout by Otter Slides, Merchant, Green, Opeongo and then the river to Victoria Lake. So my early training was from the very top men. George Markel was the other guide, and that meant there were two of us on our first guiding trip.

The first year I guided, 1917, Tom Salmon was in charge of the outfitting store at Highland Inn, and as a matter of course was called the head guide. He was one of the first settlers in Lake of Bays. He became a well-known outdoorsman, made canoes (bark canoes), and snowshoes, and was an expert fly fisherman. His father had been champion fly caster of England. I was in the party in 1927 when he gave Tom Clark his *new* fly rod, as he did not plan any more trips. He would not part with his old one, which had been his father's. The new one he had purchased on a trip back to England in 1892.

I am going to try and name the guides I have known, but will no doubt miss some. Many I never did have a trip with.

The four Mays' brothers, Bob, Fred, Dan and Ernest, along with a cousin, Al May, and his son George, all worked for many years at Tanamakoon. At time of writing George is still hale and hearty, though well into his nineties.

Others included three McLennan boys, Angus, Jack and Archie, two McCaffery men, Archie and George, Charlie McCann, George Bell, two brothers named Fetterly, a man named Goldsby Gouldie, Dan Silver, Sam Hollingshead and Albert, Gus and Roy (son of Gus) Cockram. These men were all from Huntsville.

From Dwight came four Hawk men, Lorne, Jack, Claude and Wilbur, Norm and Wilbur Gouldie, Williard, Wally and Earl Woodcock, Harry Corbett, Taylor Bradley, Frank Keown and Bert Porter.

Out of West Guilford there were Will and Wes Boice, Harry Horseley and Norm Linton and from the eastern side of the Park, Mac Richardson, George Wade, Tom Ruddy, Jack and Steve Ryan, Leo Dooner, Mike McInnerny and a man named O'Brien.

Charlie and Ed Skuce were from the east side of the Park, Barrys Bay. They guided mostly at the girl's camp, Northway Lodge. Another Skuce boy, John, came later.

The Indians from Golden Lake; Paul Tenniscoe and his three sons, Bill, Joe and Seymour, two men, brothers named Benoit, two named Joe Lavellee (one was called Hay Lake Joe) and John Parks.

Smith Cochrane, my brother and myself were from Kearney. These are guides that I knew in the hey day period involving the few years after the First World War. There have been a great many more, including many college students, who acted as guides, but names escape me. Besides they were just there a short while. I should mention that the first college guide, Alex Bruen and his father, Americans, were granted the first lease issued on Cache Lake.

I do like to brag that I guided several trips with my father and one of my boys. Too, I worked with all my three brothers, two sons and a couple of grandsons.

Superintendents

There have been a number of stories or histories written about Algonquin Park, but very little mention is made of the different Superintendents. I am going to try and put down my recollections of those men who guided the destiny of the Park.

The first man in charge was Peter Thompson. He died only a little over a year after taking office. His successor was John Simpson, who too had only three years until his early death. These two men had held office before I was born, let alone worked in the Park. So what I know of these men would be strictly hearsay. I will have to start with G.W. Bartlett, who was there when I first knew of Algonquin Park.

There are very few who will remember Geo. Bartlett, but to me, when I think of years away back, he is the person that mostly comes to mind. He had been a scaler* and had a reputation of being able to handle gangs of men. Since the Park was still quite new, and a great number of trappers still held a grudge for having their trapping grounds taken away, it was expected that whoever was in charge would have some difficult times.

His father had been a pugilist in England, and I believe he had first intended to follow his father's profession, but he changed his mind, came to Canada and worked in the woods. A story involving Bartlett concerns a lumber camp where things had gone sour. The foreman was having trouble with the crew, who had almost taken over the camp. Bartlett was asked to go and try to put everything back in order, with the warning that the men were in a fighting mood. He made the trip, and all he asked for was two or three

---

*The man who measured, for Government or Company, the volume of cut, merchantable wood.

men to keep the crowd off his back. The man who told the story to my father was one of the men who had fought the rear guard. After a fast and, for a while, furious fight, the gang of more than thirty men were subdued and all was well on that front.

During his tenure of office, anything that was happening, at least from the administration end, was handled by Mr. Bartlett. For several years he was in charge of the Fire Rangers. Then in 1917, when there was such a demand for cordwood, or rather for the chemicals they processed from cordwood, a gang or several gangs were put to cutting, followed by loading and shipping.

Queen's Park expected an awful lot of George Bartlett back in those days. The guides were also under his jurisdiction and at times, he was thought to be a bit on the strict side. There was a small golf course on the lawn, and no one played on Sunday. If guests wanted to fish on Sunday they went well away from headquarters. Drinking was not permitted. I think the original rules are still on the books and the amount of alcohol allowed per person was by todays standards very little. Once I remember a guide had gone on a bit of a bender. This was a highly rated guide, popular with both the guides and the guests. But his license was taken from him the next day.

For all his strict ideas, things were so very different away back then. Still he was a very highly respected and well-liked man. There are only a few of us left who remember him, but it is with deepest respect. Any one seeing him walk across the lawn in front of the hotel would not need to ask who was the Superintendent of Algonquin Park. At times I get to thinking about those far away days and always this man comes to mind. Since he held office for twenty-four years, it is hardly likely any other Superintendent will beat that record.

When he retired in 1922, we had J.W. Millar as acting Superintendent, then Mark Robinson for a couple of years, Millar again, as Superintendent this time, J.H. McDonald who only lived a few months, and again Mark Robinson took over.

J.W. Millar was well-known, as he had been with the department for many years and things went very well under his direction. What did bother some was the way he attempted to make his office appear more important than they had been used to. Too, his ideas were, while not of our line, a bit different than people had been used to when dealing with Mr. Bartlett or Mark Robinson.

J.H. McDonald had been around for several years and was well known by many of the regulars. He engineered the changes that were to make the Park more modern. Unfortunately, he died before many of his ideas could be put into effect, and it was said many times by interested people, that they would have liked to have seen what might have happened if he could have remained in office.

Mark Robinson always seemed to be around when some one was needed to take charge, and he again became acting-Superintendent following the death of J.H. McDonald. Then early in May, Frank MacDougall took over. If I seem to have more to write about the times of G.W. Bartlett and F.A. MacDougall, it is because these two were there each time men of their capabilities were needed.

MacDougall came along when things were in sort of a mess. The new ideas of McDonald were being tried, and they were not popular with everyone. Most of all, the friendly attitude that had always been felt at Cache Lake was gone. But this new man took things in his stide, took council with many of his top Rangers, let each and everyone know that things were changing in the Park, and in less than a year all was going smoothly. His coming too was the advent of air patrol, as he had the first airplane.

It was during MacDougall's term that elk were introduced, not by Bartlett as is stated in one of the Park picture stories. He introduced more vigilant patrols during trapping season, as records will show. He flew many of what are now called mercy flights. One of the things he did, though not until he was appointed Deputy Minister of Lands and Forests, was to set up trapping zones. This move he had discussed several times with Rangers and Guides and it was the start of what is now the best trapping set-up on the continent. Attempts were made, during that ten years, of bringing lake trout from lakes known to have an abundant population, to lakes that were heavily fished. Other lakes were also stocked. MacDougall was one of the few who could see, with the upsurge in summer visitors, the Park waters would be heavily fished.

It was quite natural that many of us were more than a little sorry to see him go in the summer of 1941, after being around for ten years.

We had Jim Taylor for a couple of years, son of D.J. Taylor, a former Deputy Minister of Game and Fisheries, and one of the most popular men ever to be in that division. He also flew, and was always ready to help when he could.

Then there was George Phillips, whose whole life was spent flying. He had been in the infantry in the First War, and was one of the best heavy-weight boxers. In the championship eliminations he made the finals, and was a heavy favourite to win, but just a few hours before the bout, his commission came through and as an officer he could not box with an enlisted man, so he missed becoming champion of the Canadian Army.

George Phillips was Superintendent for fifteen years and things went quite smoothly. It was during his term that most of the summer hotels were torn down, and that meant the end of another era in Algonquin. He retired in 1958 and until his death lived on his farm near Orangeville.

Phillips was followed by R.C. Passmore, Dick to most of us who had known him when he had other positions. He was there only two years, moving on to Ottawa to join a Wildlife Group.

Then V.W. Fiskar, better know simply as Yorky, came along. Yorky was also a pilot and well-known to many of us in the Park.

By this time fishermen were not allowed to land in the Park, except on just a few lakes. That ruling, I believe, came in about 1954.

When Fiskar went back to Toronto, T.W. Hueston arrived and was around for eight years; he often stated that he hoped he would never have to leave. It was he who started the idea of campers taking their garbage out of the Park.

I believe it was Hueston who decided there should be more control on timber operations. It has been mentioned a lot of times, that if logging had been as well controlled thirty years ago as it is today, there might not have been any reason to form the Wildlands League.

J.H. Lever followed Hueston, and was in charge for a couple of years, and again everything went smoothly.

John Simpson came in 1975, and is still looking after things. All seems to be going well, but with the present staff, so many men for so many different projects, I sometimes wonder what G.W. Bartlett would think of present day operations. Years ago the Superintendent also was the magistrate, who sat on cases of infringements committed within the Park boundary. This was discontinued during the early thirties.

I have worked with all these men who have been in charge except the first two, and that was before my time. Let's hope that whoever is in charge will see to it that Algonquin Park is kept as closely as possible to the concept and plan set down by the Park's early creators.

Frank MacDougall

I was one of the many people who received an invitation to attend the ceremony at the West Gate in Algonquin Park, when that portion of Highway 60 that goes through the Park received a new name, *The Frank MacDougall Highway*.

It is a fitting tribute to the man who was Superintendent of the Park for several years, and his work was so good, that on the retirement of Walter Gain, the then Premier, Mitchell Hepburn, jumped party lines and asked Frank to come to Toronto and take over as Deputy Minister. Later we will have some remarks on his long career with the Lands and Forests, now known as the Ministry of Natural Resources.

There were the usual greetings and conversations from many of the gathering, as many were renewing acquaintances some going back since before the last war.

John Simpson opened the meeting. He welcomed the visitors, and explained a bit about his role in Algonquin Park, as he is the Superintendent. He called on the Deputy Minister, Dr. Keith Reynolds, who told us something of the long and dedicated service Frank MacDougall had given, not only to the Park, but to all of Ontario. Simpson then introduced the speaker, Paul Yakabuski, M.P.P. for Renfrew South, also the assistant to the Minister, the Hon. Leo Bernier, who could not attend. Since Paul had lived in Barrys Bay on the east side of the Park, he was well acquainted with the welcome changes that had taken place after Frank had taken charge. He had a well prepared address, and spoke of the way wildlife had increased with the new policies, especially for fur bearing animals. He a bit jokingly referred to the many expert poachers he had known in the early days, and it was just a little embarrassing when so many turned and looked at me.

Finally, the tape was cut by Frank's two daughters, and Mrs. MacDougall was presented with two handsomely carved beaver decorations.

It did not seem that it was almost forty-five years since Frank MacDougall came to Algonquin Park. He had served overseas in the First World War on the infantry, and on his return took service with Land and Forests, or perhaps it was called Ontario Forestry Branch then. He was stationed at Sault Ste. Marie. Airplanes were just coming into use with that Department, and I believe George Phillips, then a pilot, later to become Park Superintendent, taught Frank how to fly. We do know that when he came to the Park, we also had the first airplane to be stationed there, and he was the pilot.

Matters had not been going well in the Park. Following the retirement of G. Bartlett in 1923, things had been getting into a bit of a muddle. In the early thirties a chap named McDonald had been appointed Superintendent, and he had planned many changes. One was to have only one group of Rangers. Up to that time there were perhaps twenty-five Park Rangers whose duty was to protect game. Then in the summer months an equal, perhaps greater number of Fire Rangers were appointed, whose duty it was to keep trails clear, and protect the area from fires. Most in the two groups were on the best of terms, but when it was announced that there would be only one group, with perhaps a few extra hired men in the summer, there was a bit of hard feeling between the two categories of Rangers. Then the summer visitors began to take sides, some with the Fire Rangers, and some with the Park Rangers. You never knew what kind of an argument you could get into when you started to talk about the new ideas for Algonquin Park. The Fire Rangers did not trust the Park Rangers, the summer visitors did not trust either faction, and the guides got so they did not trust anyone.

McDonald, as he was known, died less than a year after he had taken over as District Forester and Superintendent of the Park, and Frank MacDougall came to the Park just a few months after McDonald's death. Paul Yakabuski mentioned in his speech that we were fortunate that it was a man like Frank MacDougall who was the go-between during that transition.

Algonquin Park, especially around Cache Lake, was such a friendly place. We did not have a road then, and everyone came in on the train. But I do not think any one spot could have as many friendly people as there were on Cache Lake, and this included the guests at the Highland Inn, the C.N.R. hotel since demolished.

It may have been that people on holidays in such a lovely setting could forget all their troubles. It may be that on quiet lakes and such lovely shorelines, people just felt friendly. (It has been suggested that perhaps the close association with the guides made the people pleasant). But whatever the reason, I still think of Cache Lake as a wonderfully friendly spot.

I have been at other gatherings, where Frank was lauded for the work he had done, but no one mentioned what some of us think was one thing he did so very well, which was restoring that feeling of good fellowship that had been missing in the Park when so many were finding fault.

One of the things many of us admired him for was the fact that he gave credit to people who had lived in the woods for many years, of having gained a bit of knowledge. The last few years, unless you were college trained, it was not conceded that you knew much about the woods. Too, the trappers can thank Frank MacDougall for Ontario having the best set-up for trappers anywhere in the world. We had been asking for many years for trapping zones to be established, but were always told it could not be done. Shortly after Frank went to Queen's Park to take over as Deputy Minister, the idea was put into effect, and everyone knows the results. By the way, the later Dr. William Harkness must be given credit for being behind the idea, when he was Chief of Fish and Wildlife.

Hunters got a favour from him too. We used to be allowed one day each year to meet with the standing committee and blow our tops about things we would like changed. Hunter groups complained there were getting to be too many hunt camp leases. There was a ruling that they must be at least one and one half miles apart, but as many know, anyone with some political help could get around that. Several of us were called into his office, we told our story, and a survey was made, the results being that no more hunt camp leases were issued.

At the conclusion of the ceremonies, I felt very proud to have been part of a gathering that in a small way did a bit to honour a man who had done so much for Algonquin Park, and for all of Ontario. Only thing, too bad this had not been thought of while he was around, so he could have appreciated it.

Trappers

These accounts will be about early trappers, where they trapped, and where they came from. The ones I will talk about are mostly trappers from the area in Haliburton County, from Dorset through to West Guilford. It also happens that most of them were somehow or other related to my family. First I will give you the names and then later I will tell you where they trapped. There is Isaac Bice who was my grandfather, Ham Bice who was his brother, and Johnny Archer; they trapped together. There was Jim Sawyer, who was an uncle, and he had two sons Henry and Ben. He also had a number of grandsons who have kept on trapping. Durland Redner was one of the early trappers, and a man named Jake Clancy, my Dad and his two brothers. There was a man named Tim Holland, who was one of the earliest settlers in Kearney, and had a camp on Eagle Lake, a man named Harvey also from this area, had a camp on Tims Lake, it was called Shoe Lake then. Then, there were a number of Sawyers from the Haliburton, North Haliburton area, that trapped in the southeast corner near the present boundary.

My Grandad, Isaac Bice, supposedly was the first white man that went up the river they called the Pine (it is called the Tim River now), from Big Trout Lake, then called White Trout, up to Roseberry where he built a camp in either 1870 or 1871. I was at the camp in 1911, at least what was left of it, and now I am possibly the only person that knows just where it was. That was at Roseberry Lake, and Grandad trapped there for many years.

This is a matter of record, so I might as well add it. In the fall of 1893 the trappers had been notified, during the summer I guess, about the establishment of Algonquin Park, and suggested that they find some place else to trap. There was nothing done to compensate them in any way, they were just told to leave. On the other hand Tim Holland, who had the camp on Eagle Lake, had the camp purchased from him by the government, and it was used for a number of years as a Ranger's cabin. I helped tear it down in 1917.

My grandfather had met an Indian on Big Trout Lake. The Indian was in bad shape, and grandfather took him in, fed him and fixed him up. He told grandfather there was a stream coming in in the west side and if you followed it up far enough you would come to a nice lake and there was some good trapping in that area. My grandfather followed his advice and trapped there for a long time. As I mentioned before, they had been informed that it was now a Park, and they did not know what to do, as their traps were in the woods, so they went in anyway. My grandfather had gotten to his camp in the mid-day, and was just sitting on the bench outside wondering what it was all about, when Dan Ross came along. Dan Ross was one of the early Park Rangers, and there was nothing done except that he informed my grandfather that he could not trap and he had to take his traps and leave. I do not know how far he went, but he did take his outfit and moved out. So whether it's worth talking about, or not, sometimes, just for the sake of argument, we sort of brag that our grandfather was the first poacher apprehended in Algonquin Park.

The boys from this side never went over the divide on the part of the Park that goes down to the Opeongo, that was sort of left for the Indians from the east side, who had trapped there since the time there was ever any trapping.

Jim Sawyer was related to my grandfather by marriage, and a couple of years after grandfather came into the area, Jim built a camp on Eagle Lake. I had been in the camp many times years ago. We found some bottles there that are now in a museum in Boston, these bottles are highly prized as they are the old blown variety. Jim Sawyer also had a camp on Misty Lake and I had been in it the year that we hunted deer in that part of the country.

Jake Clancy's widow married again and lived only a mile from us. She was the type of lady we called Grandma Jones, so you know what we thought of her. Clancy had had camps on McCraney Lake, Mink Creek and Rainy Lake. At that time it wasn't McCraney Lake, it was Moose Lake. Towards the end he sort of got tired of trapping and sold his trapline to Jim Sawyer's sons, Ben and Hank, and they trapped there for quite a long time.

Then there was a man named Durland Redner, I went to school with his children. Redner had a camp on Horn Lake, which is two portages north of Carolyn Lake (Source Lake). His camp was standing in 1934-35. It was built of cedar with a scoop roof. The lake is now known as Linda's Lake. I don't know who Linda was, but the lake is shaped like a horn, so they called it Horn Lake in those days.

I mentioned that Tim Holland trapped on Eagle Lake. It wasn't so much of a trapping camp, as Tim would often go in there and catch an awful lot of fish. In those days there wasn't too much worry about seasons or nets, and they would drive in, in the winter time. I talked to one man that had made a trip with Holland and with three lifts of a net they had all the fish they could put in the box on the jumper, which was made of twelve inch boards, four feet wide and eight feet long. They just went down and filled the box with fish and came out, and everybody in the area had fish. Tim Holland's house was just about three miles from Kearney.

Another trapper by the name of Harvey, used to trap up on Tim's Lake, and he often met my grandfather down river.

I have mentioned the Sawyers. There were two of them that trapped south of Algonquin Park around Dividing Lake and Coon Lake. After the Park was established, several years afterwards, my father and grandfather bought their trapping rights for a very small sum (it would be in these days), and they trapped in that country, especially in Lake Louise, for a great many years. That area was taken into Algonquin park in 1913, but Dad often talked about what a nice country it was to travel in, with many lakes and small portages.

In those times the travelling was mostly one trip in the spring where they trapped beaver, maybe a bear or two, otter and muskrat. They would leave home just as soon as the ice was out and they figured they would be away for a month. Then they would come home and get busy at what they called in those days, farming.

In the fall they would leave, generally the first weekend in October, and do nearly all the trapping in October. The fur sale was at Minden, and the fur sales were held on November 7th. The trappers all wanted to be out for those fur sales. I have since been in Minden, of course, but what a wonderful sight it must have been back then to see those people all coming down the Gull River in their canoes with the furs. They would stretch their own little tents and then barter with the fur buyers the next day.

I will remember always when my Dad, his brothers, and Grandfather, came home from the woods. Dad trapped sometimes with his father, sometimes with one of his brothers; and most times by the pickup round they would not have the fur stretched or dried, so they would come up to our place, and I can still see it all quite clearly.

Up on the hill behind the house they built a fire, the same place every year, and they had some benches rigged up, or some logs, and I will recall as long as I live, going up there and sitting spellbound as I listened to them, and watched them stretch fur. It may have been about then that I decided that I was going to be a trapper, and, rightly or wrongly I did it.

I find it interesting that there were no beaver in Algonquin Park when it was established, and had not been for several years. The last fur sale that my Dad could remember much about, 1892, was the year before the Park was established, and of the several dozen trappers there he was the only man that had more than two beaver. Many didn't have any beaver at all, and that's trapping a month in open water, and an awful lot in the area we now call Algonquin Park, where there is numerous beaver. For some reason or other the beaver cycle had just about run out. On one occasion some of the old timers were talking about when the Park was established, and amongst them they only knew six places in Algonquin Park where there was beaver. Today it is not unusual to see that many group together on one lake.

The early trappers caught a lot of mink. My Dad told me the first year he came into the woods, which was 1888, Jim Sawyer, instead of cutting across his camp on Butt Lake, wanted to talk to my Grandad, and came over to Roseberry Lake. Grandad was out on the line but Dad was there. And Jim Sawyer on the day before and that day had picked up 18-20 mink. Dad remembers helping him skin them that night, and that was the result of just two days travelling and not a great many traps. They also caught a great bunch of marten. Uncle Will and Uncle Wes, who were my Dad's brothers, in one fall trapping in Divine Township, with only thirty traps, had caught besides mink, sixty-eight or seventy marten.

There were fisher, quite a few fisher, but there seemed to be a bigger population down around Catfish Lake because my Uncle Ham Bice and Johnny Archer, came out every Fall with twelve to twenty fisher, as many as half the other trappers had combined. They seemed to have a pocket of fisher that didn't run out on them.

They had a few muskrat, but they weren't worth a great deal. Some otter, as a matter of fact quite a few otter, and there were a few raccoon, a few bears, and maybe a fox or two.

I also remember my one Uncle telling me, that one year somebody got a lynx, and the next year several people got lynx. From then on for a number of years, until apparently the cycle ran out, every trapper came home with two or three lynx from the area that is now Algonquin Park, until they disappeared again.

So those are the trappers I knew, and they were all related to me in some way or other, and all from about the one area. They trapped the southwestern — western side of Algonquin Park, and south of it. The other side, the east side, was left mostly to Indians. I don't know about the north side but it did take these people two days travel, if the weather was good, to get from their homes in West Guilford up to Big Trout Lake.

How nice it must have been when fifteen or twenty trappers would travel together and the first night camp together. Everybody with his own little tent, everybody with his own cooking fire, and it must have been pretty nice travelling with a small bark canoe, and a very minimum outfit. But when they got farther in on the big lakes they would spread out and each would go to his own trapping ground. Occasionally they would have a hand sleigh, on which they would put their little bark canoe, and then their packs and other stuff would go in the canoe. They would put the rope over their shoulder and travel for two or three days to get in to where they wanted to trap. They would trap for a while on the crust and then when the ice went out they would use their canoe and go home.

One story I like to tell involves two uncles of my father's, both married to my grandfather's sisters. They were coming up a long hill down by Dividing Lake and apparently it had been a logging road and it was well cut out. Vantclief was ahead and a man name Grozelle, a Frenchman, was right behind him. Vantclief got to the top of the hill first, but didn't go quite far enough to give Grozelle a chance to have his sleigh on upper ground. The second man thought it was alright and he just dropped the rope and puffed a little bit. All of a sudden the sleigh started backwards and hit a tree and turned around and went right back down to the foot of the hill on their snowshoe tracks. Vantclief was having a great laugh when his brother-in-law turned to him and said, *'Well Daniel, you can laugh. I've been thinking of it for a long time. I'm through trapping. I'm going to buy me a yoke of cattle and farm.'* And he never went trapping again.

Rangers

This will be about the Park Rangers as I remember them, going back to 1910-11. I have read a lot of the early writings about Algonquin Park, but if all my research is correct, and I have put it down correctly, the first four Park Rangers were Steve Waters, Dan Ross, John Gorman and Tim O'Leary.

Not long afterwards they started taking on more and there was Albert Ranger, he was from Mattawa, and he was known as Albear Rangey. I never met him, but I met one of his sons and he was a wonderful chap. Speaking of the Ranger Family, travellers and fishermen in later years who were lucky enough to meet Pete Ranger were always sure of a good story, or if time permitted, many of them. Pete was a great story teller, and had a great fund to draw from, especially about early times. His camp was near Kiosk, though he had been retired for many years.

Other early Rangers included Bob Balfour, Wm. Marshall, Eli Donjini, Nelson Bangs, Jim Sawyer, George Stringer, Tom Watty, Bud Calaghan, Mark Robinson, Jim Shields, Jack Stringer, Jack Culhane, Fred Bice, Bob Patterson, Ernie Geates, Pete and Telesphore Ranger, Jim Hughes, Andy Grant, Dave Valentine, Jack Christie, Art Briggs, Alex Watson, Jim Bartlett, Zeff Naddon, a man named Frank Robichaud, who died all alone on Three Mile Lake, Bill Mooney, Dan Stringer, Ed Goddard, Charlie Brewer, Archie Benn, Jack Gervais, and Martin Newell. Now there may have been a few Rangers I have missed, but those were the ones that were quite active until the changeover in the late thirties when they decided that the Rangers would become both Park Rangers and Fire Rangers.

Tom McCormick and Jerry Kennedy were appointed Chief Rangers. In the mid-twenties there had been a mild shake-up, and Bill Lewis and Jim Shields were appointed Chief Rangers. The names of those who became Park

Rangers I do not remember,there were a number and they kept being moved around. I am going to try and tell you where these Rangers ranged, along about the time of the First World War.

Steve Waters was one of the early ones, and he knew his birds. He had a Degree in Mining from the University of Toronto. He kept quite a diary, which has been very helpful to the people writing histories of Algonquin Park.

Dan Ross who was the first Park Ranger that I met, in 1912, was the same great river driver mentioned in Glengarry Schooldays.* Big Dan was also the builder of the first Ranger's cabin on Eagle Lake. It was used up to 1948-49 as a sleep camp. When it was torn down, I found underneath the floor a broadaxe,* quite possibly the one he had used in building his reputation as an expert axeman. I put a handle on it and hewed many, many, sills for cottages in Algonquin Park. The last cottage that I built, I inadvertently left the broadaxe there, and I got in touch with the man and said I'll come down and fetch it. The man died that winter and his wife sold the camp, and when I went for the broadaxe the people claimed that they had bought it with the camp. Unfortunately, I didn't tell them that there was a bit of history attached.

Tim O'Leary was the first Chief Ranger in the Park. Tim's Lake was named after him, as was the Tim River, once known as the Pine River, because it has such a wonderful stand of pines.

George Goddard was posted down on the eastern part, south of Opeongo Lake, for a great many years. I met Eli Danjini there. Eli and George had worked together for a good many years. Finally, Goddard was sent to Rainy Lake after Dan Ross retired. My many visits with Danjini were at Crotch Lake.

Bob Balfour, from Arnprior, used to range in and around White Trout Lake, Big Trout they call it now. He was in the Park when I came because he and my Dad worked together quite a bit. William Marshall of Emsdale took his place when I first was around Brule Lake.

Another Ranger of those times was Nelson Bangs from Mattawa, but he was over in the north country and I often met him around Headquarters.

Jim Sawyer, who was one of the early trappers, was offered a job as Park Ranger, and I believe all his term of being a Ranger he spent up on Manitou and Tea Lake in the northwest corner of the Park. I didn't get the names quite in order here, because Tom Watty was his partner. I knew them both well and I have been in their former camps, since they have gone, many times.

Then there was George Stringer from Killaloe, and he was the Ranger at Brule Lake when my Dad came on the force in 1910. That first winter my Dad was with Stringer they travelled from Brule Lake through to Misty Lake up to

---

*by author Ralph Connor, an excellent account of early Ontario.
*Short axe with 12 in. blade bevelled on one side like a chisel, for hewing masts, square timber, railway ties.

Eagle Lake, out that way. George too became a bit old and they sent him down to a nicer spot on Rock Lake. In the spring of 1923, and he knew better, he went across the ice on the early frost, and when he started back, they told him, 'that ice isn't going to carry you back George, it is going fast'. But he tried it and he drowned only a couple of hundred yards from his camp.

I don't know what year Bud Callaghan came on, but I think it was maybe 1907 or 1908. I knew Bud slightly but I later worked with his sons. Bud Callaghan lived at Dwight and reached 95 years of age.

Mark Robinson was from Barrie and I believe Bud Callaghan was from there too. They came on about the same time. Robinson I got to know very, very well. As a matter of fact, I would say next to my father, and maybe my uncles, I respected Mark Robinson. He always had time to talk to us young lads. The first year we were down there if we wanted something to do, we would go over to Mark Robinson's camp. Those were the first summers I worked in the Park, at 14 and 15 years of age, and he always had time, it didn't matter what he was doing, he could stop and talk to the boys.

Mark went overseas in the First World War. He was a Major in the 57th Battalion. He was wounded and since he was too old for trench warfare, they sent him back. He went back on the Park staff again and was once appointed Superintendent. Mark completed his term as a Ranger, ending up at Headquarters. He retired and lived to be well up in years, and I've always treasured my friendship with him. Incidentally, he has a daughter that has written books on Algonquin Park and Tom Thomson, and she and I were and are very good friends.

Chief Ranger Jim Shields was from Whitney and occupied a vast area greatly occupied by Indians. He was well liked by everybody. Jack Stringer, a cousin of George Stringer, also from Killaloe, came on the force just about the same time as my father did. He worked down on the eastern side when I met him and he was then in partnership with Eli Danjini.

Jack Culhane, I believe was a brother-in-law of Jack Stringer's, when I knew him over on Lake Travers. He was a very obliging man and a very nice person to meet.

I well remember Bob Patterson and Ernie Geates, for many years the Rangers at Moose Lake, now know as McCraney.

Jim Hughes was at Kiosk for many years. When he left the park, Hughes went into the grocery store business in Sudbury.

Another Ranger, Andy Grant, was at Cedar Lake most of the time. I met him at Headquarters and became friendly with him.

Then there was Dave Valentine from South River, my Dad's partner for a great many years. Before Dave, Dad had been paired off with Bob White, also from Kearney. As a matter of fact, descendants of his are still here. And then there was Jack Christie, and after they split up the beats, Christie and Valentine had the northend and Dad and Bill Mooney had the southend. Ranger Art Briggs was around Joe Lake for a great many years, a really nice man. Once he was at his ranger's cabin on Island Lake, maybe two hundred yards from the Minissjing Hotel, when all of a sudden there was a great deal of screaming and Briggs, who was a returned soldier, jumped in his canoe and paddled over. He was told that a canoe had upset and one of the passengers hadn't surfaced. They had some flashlights, and were out wading, and he dove down into twenty-two feet of water and found this girl and brought her up on the dock. He was the only person there that knew anything about artificial respiration, using the old method, he did revive the girl. He was decorated for it, which he richly deserved.

Now then there was a man named Alex Watson. Alex had been a Fire Ranger and camp foreman before he was made an active Park Ranger. It was about that time officials decided it was necessary to follow the railroad's route through the Park and eliminate brush, close to the track, as there were too many fires caused by shooting sparks from the engines as they pushed up steep grades. Alex was in charge and I worked for him two summers. Now I never saw him on a drive, but he was considered one of the best teamsters you could take in the woods and it was a treat to watch him using an axe. He didn't have to go round a tree, whichever hand he picked up the axe in, he could use. Sometimes I pride myself on being an axeman, I've seen lots of others, but Alex Watson has to be the best axeman I ever saw.

Jim Bartlett, he was the son of the Superintendent, was with Mark Robinson at Joe Lake for many years. I knew him very well. He had studied some taxidermy and decided they should have a specimen of each of the Park animals mounted. Jim did it and they looked very well in the office at Headquarters.

There was a man named Zeff Neddon, an awfully nice chap, and he was down on Trout Lake. He was there when they started building cottages.

Now there is another man named Robichaud, and I forget his first name. I met him several times when I was guiding over on the northline and became very good friends. Finally he was shifted up to Three Mile Lake, that's up near Manitou Lake, and he hadn't come out for his supplies or for his mail, and they discovered when they went in to look for him, the poor chap lying dead on the floor. They figured he had been dead for two weeks when they found him.

A First War veteran, Bill Mooney, came on the Park staff, and was with my Dad for a number of years. Bill had been a carpenter and he did a lot of building around the lakes in th Park.

Dan Stringer, who was the last of the old Park Rangers, came on after the First War, and he was the son of Jack Stringer. Dan got to be one of the best liked Rangers in the Park. Whenever any VIP's came to the Park and wanted a guide, they would always send for Dan Stringer. He died only a few years ago, one of the finest men you could ever wish to meet.

Then there was Ned Goddard, a nephew of George's whose post was at Rainy Lake for a while. Yet another Park Ranger was Brewer, who was at Basin Depot.

Also there was Jack Gervais, whose one daughter lives in Kearney and a son is in Huntsville. One of Dr. Case's books is mostly about Jack Gervais and his Park experiences. There was a man who was up at North Tea Lake, I believe his name was Edwards, but he Park Ranged there and I saw him several times.

Finally there was a man named Martin Newell. He was on several beats, but he wound up his tenure as the Gateman when the road first went through in 35-36. I guess that sounds like a long time ago to people that are now going into the Park. To those of us that were there then, that was the beginning of the end of Algonquin Park as we had known it.

When Frank McDougall came there some major changes occurred; all the men were called just Rangers and that included both Park and Fire Rangers. Since McDougall had the airplane for looking for fires, they didn't need quite so many men.

There are still a few Rangers, I don't know whether they call them that now or Wardens. Of course, when I think of the Park and go back into any of these lakes, and I think of the Rangers that were there then, it does make for very nice memories.

The Last of the
Old Park Rangers

The death in Sundridge of Dan Stringer removed the last of the real old Park Rangers. I believe there is still one of the older Rangers, living in retirement, but Dan Stringer was on the Park staff during the tenure of the late G.W. Bartlett. Since Mr. Bartlett retired in 1922, that makes it quite a long time ago.

If anyone has had the privilege of reading Mrs. Addison's book on the early years in Algonquin Park, and has seen the picture of a group of Rangers, taken with Mr. Bartlett at the time of his retirement party, Dan is the young man sitting on the steps.

I first met Dan in the spring of 1915. There was a gang of men taken on during the summer months in the Park, and their work was to clear the brush and dead wood ninety feet back from the rails on the old railroad. I had worked on that project in the summer of 1914, and back again the following year. On this gang in 1915 there were several boys from Killaloe, amongst them Dan Stringer. Like myself, his father was a Park Ranger. He was seldom called Dan, as in common with many of the boys of his family, he had a nickname, and that simple name was 'Mud'. I believe there were about five from Killaloe about my own age, which was then fifteen. But Dan was a few years older and we were more than a little jealous of him, as he was allowed to sit in during the card games and we were not. Too, he owned and proudly wore a gold watch chain, of the type which were very popular then.

Like all young boys of that era, as you grew you learned to use an axe and saw, as well as other tools used in the woods, and it was expected that everyone would know how to paddle a canoe.

That Fall many of us went into war work, and those old enough joined the army and went overseas. Dan was one of the latter, and the first I heard of him after the war was that he had been appointed to the Park staff. As I was guiding all summer in the Park, it was natural I saw him many times. Since as that picture I mentioned shows him to be much the youngest ranger, he was subjected to many jibes and practical jokes by his older co-workers. These he took in good part, and I do not think he had a bad friend on the staff, or amongst the many guides then working in that area.

Dan had had his share of lumbering. On both sides of his family, the men were known as skilled woodsmen. There is a story that was told of the first winter he spent in the lumber camp, where the walking boss was an uncle. Like many other young men, or perhaps I should say boys, Dan got into a bit of mischief now and then. His uncle felt it was his duty to sort of act as a guardian, even to the point of corporal punishment. The story says that the uncle got the worst of it. But as I said, it may only be a story.

Being young, and no family of his own, Dan was sent to a lot of places. In the summer he often worked around Headquarters. Since the Park Staff had the only team of horses, they were often hired to take groups back into the woods to a couple of lakes that were not far from the road. It was particularly pleasant when Dan was the driver, for his stories and friendly talk kept everyone happy and amused. He forever seemed to be in a happy mood, and in all the years I knew him, and that has been a long while, I never saw him out of sorts, or heard him speak unkindly about another person.

Once he told me about being caught on the woods during freeze up. He and another Ranger were at the McIntish Marsh shelter hut, and this other man got really sick, I believe with quinsy (inflammation of the throat). Dan was in quite a state, as they were a long ways from the railroad. But the man did recover, and they made their way out.

There was another thing Dan did not like to talk about too much, though he did relate it to Audrey Saunders when she was writing her story of the Park.

This happened in a lake north of Kiosk. Pete Ranger, one of the older members of the Park staff, was fighting a wolf in the water. He had caught the animal out in the lake, and had broken one paddle, but the wolf was almost gone when Dan, having seen what was going on from the other side of the lake, came in a motor boat to help. In spite of Pete's pleas of no help, Dan produced a revolver and shot the wolf, which immediately sank. A lot of time was spent trying to find it with a drag, but it was never recovered. Rangers were then allowed to keep the bounty on wolves, and $25.00 was a lot of money forty years ago.

One summer, more than fifty years ago, Camp Amek Statten used to have a sort of day long pageant, and a lot of people attended, from other lakes. This meant a trip of several miles, as there were no roads then, just paddle and portage. Dan had gotten quite friendly with one of the cottage groups, and promised to take some of them to this pageant. He had worked one Sunday, and this was to be his day off. The morning of the pageant the acting Superintendent sent for Dan and told him that he would be expected to take his family to the *Big Event*. Dan explained that he had other plans, and since he had a day coming, this was it. The Superintendent informed him that that did not matter, he was to take his family. I was there, with another cottage group, and I saw Dan, and he did not have the Super's family. Most of us were more than a little bit pleased.

Twenty-five years ago, or thereabouts, the department purchased several of the old outdated hotels, and tore them down. Dan was appointed Superintendent in charge, and just about finished his tenure in the Park at that work. Most of the old Park Rangers had been retired, there had been a big change in the policy of the Park, and one of the few you could meet and talk to about old times was Dan Stringer. Eventually, and I do not recall the year, he too went the route of older men and began many enjoyable years of retirement.

We met many times, usually at Lodge, and on almost every occasion we would talk about what it was like in the Park more than sixty years ago. Many times we made plans to get together and compare our old snapshots, but this never did get to happen.

EDITOR'S NOTE: *Famous Canadian canoeist, Omer Stringer, co-author with Dan Gibson of 'Canoeist's Manual' (Amethyst) is a surviving brother of Dan Stringer.*

Mercy Flight,
circa 1918

This can hardly be called a mercy flight, as there were no planes around, but a well managed train and canoe trip no doubt saved two lives.

As I said, it was 1918. Nominigan Camp on Smoke Lake was full of guests and as most of them were yearly visitors, everyone was having a good summer. Nominigan Camp was run by the G.T.R., along with Minnising Camp on Big Island Lake, and the main hotel, Highland Inn on Cache Lake.

One of the guests was an American lady, who along with her husband and ten year old son occupied one of the cottages. The lady was also expecting a baby, but they liked Algonquin Park so much they felt they would be back home in plenty of time for the blessed event.

Also among the guests was a doctor from St. Catherines, and he too had his family. The doctor later became Mayor of his little city, and his daughter marries a famous oarsman, and their son also made his mark rowing.

I do not know entirely what happened. If I ever did know I have forgotten, but the lady took sick, this doctor was called, and he did not like what he found, as birth was imminent and the unfortunate woman would of a necessity, need an operation.

Now there were no phones, or at least what there was wouldn't have been too good. Fortunately this doctor somehow or other, made arrangements for a special train to have a clear track, with necessary equipment and nurses. I do not recall if the train was made up in Toronto, or St. Catherines, but it did have all necessary clearance, and made a record run to Algonquin Park.

Headquarters then was at Algonquin Park Station, and there was a road of sorts that enabled a stage to get to Nominigan. But as this would be slow, the train was stopped at Joe Lake, and the nurses and all they brought were taken in by canoes. At this time there was not a single out-board motor in the Park, so it meant paddling. Enough canoes were obtained, so that they would not need to be carried over the portage between Canoe and Smoke Lake. From the train at Joe Lake station it was perhaps 200 yards to where the canoes waited. When the party reached the portage from Canoe to Smoke Lake more guides were waiting, and everything and everybody was hurried to Smoke Lake, about one quarter of a mile, and there more canoes with two guides each were waiting for the final run to the camp.

Everything that could be done to be ready for the final chapter had been arranged by the doctor. The lights in the cottages were acetyline gas, which, if anyone remembers, did not give a very bright light. There were no gasoline lanterns at that time, but all the flashlights, and there were not as many then as now, had been gathered, and several provided light for the operation. A dining room table had been made ready, the doctor was waiting and minutes after the nurses and instruments arrived things got underway.

At this time, I was away on a fishing trip, but if I had been at the Inn it is doubtful if I would have been involved, as there were many guides to choose from, and for such a trip the older men were used.

The operation was a success, and I saw the baby as a boy of six or seven a few years afterwards. The doctor and his family continued to spend their summer holidays at Nominigan, until the camps closed, late in the twenties or early thirties. For a few summers the incident was a favourite topic of conversation. All is well that ends well, and such an operation today would be of small record, but the way it was handled then, with the train all the way with a clear track, and the way the nurses and equipment were taken in to Nominigan, made for a very good story.

Just before the last war this doctor made a trip to Algonquin Park. Then he came all the way by car, and wanted to go over and see Nominigan Camp. He was accompanied by his daughter, and it befell my good luck to take them by canoe and portage from Cache Lake to Smoke Lake. The camp was privately owned, and it had been sold after a fire destroyed the cottages. He was even then a bit dismayed at the changes taking place following the building of the road.

This was the first time I had met this doctor, and I had first hand the story of the event that had happened twenty or more years ago. He did not attach too much importance to his skill as a surgeon, but he still talked of the way the railroad co-operated getting the train through, and of the help from the Park officials and the guides.

Rangers Dan Stringer *(left)* and Jack Stringer *(right)*.

Wagon laden with canoes — on portage, Algonquin Park, *circa* 1897.

Jim Sawyer stretching beaver. Sawyer built his trapping camp on Eagle Lake (Butt), in 1872. He became a ranger in 1898.

| Guides and fishermen, Crow River, 1927. Tom Salmon, with whiskers, *right centre*. | Park Rangers in front of boarding house at time of retirement of Supt. G.W. Bartlett *(Bartlett 2nd from left)*. |

Guides, Steve and Jack Ryan, Whitney, 1927.

Taylor Statten

Mark Robinson. Taken at Cache Lake around 1933-34, with Sheeko, famous sleigh dog of Ranger Claude MacFarlane.

School children with teacher Edith Chapple,
Rain Lake 1903.

Old shelter hut on the Opeongo.

The original Portage Store, Canoe
Lake — a great contrast to the large
service centre at the site to-day.

Old driving camp at foot of
Shippigew Lake.

Algonquin Park Headquarters at Cache Lake, about 1900. The Superintendent's home *(left)* and staffhouse *(right)*.

Hotel Algonquin was a rustic structure situated back from the railway station on a hill overlooking Joe Lake.

This cottage on Brule Lake now owned by Dr. Edmund Kase Jr.
was one of the first built in the Park   *(by the Barnet Lumber Company)*.

Algonquin Park Waterways

During the late twenties someone decided that there should be some changes made in the names of the lakes in Algonquin Park. In nineteen twenty-eight the boundary between Nipissing and Parry Sound Districts had been surveyed and with the resultant (Sky Line) a new aerial map was made of Algonquin Park and the surrounding sections. The maps were quite accurate, and a very decided improvement on any previous map. Then came the job of changing names. Seems like they wanted a name for one of the larger lakes to be named after the township in which it was located. Too, some of the lakes had names that were a bit confusing with lakes of the same name in other sections of the Province, some of them not that far away. While the idea may have been sound, when the new names were announced, a lot of the romance connected with these lakes seemed to disappear. There was some dissention from some of the older visitors, but it soon died down. Many of the old timers continued to call the lakes by the names they had known them by, but there are a lot of people who visit the Park each summer, and they have known the lakes only by the new names, and it does not seem to matter.

Manitou
Lake

North Tea
Lake

Nipissing River

Catfish Lake

Madawaska River

Little

Tim Lake
Butt
Lake

Big Trout
Lake

Big Crow Lake

Little Crow
Lake

Lake Traverse

Tim River

Misty
Lake

Rain Lake

Otterslide
Lake

Opeongo
Lake

Lake
Layieille

McCraney
Lake

Burnt Island
Lake

Bonnechere

Stratton Lake

Canoe
Lake

Little Joe Lake

Lake of Two Rivers

Smoke
Lake

Cache Lake

Booth Lake

Bonnechere
Lake

Lonisa
Lake

Galeary
Lake

Pine

Madawaska Lake

LIBERTY

Big (White) Trout Lake

While this lake, originally called White Trout, is not quite in the geographical centre of Algonquin Park, it certainly is the most travelled. Two routes from the old railroad came to Big Trout. One, the most used, came in from Joe Lake by the way of Burnt Island and the Otter Slide Lakes. The other came in from Brule Lake, across McIntosh and then the long, long stretch known as McIntosh Marsh. From the east there was the trail from Merchants Lake. From the west the Petawawa and the Pine (Tim) River trails. To the north was the route down the Petawawa to Brent, and the overland trail to Lake Lamuir. Being the central lake on so many routes, many parties camp there or paddle through. There are many camping spots, and in the middle of the summer now there may be as many as a dozen or more parties there at one time. The great majority of the campers nowadays are from the several boys and girls camps. Years ago one had the feeling when White Trout was reached that you were well back in the wilderness, but now to camp on that lake is much different. There are parties on nearly every site, and when the fires are lit at night it seems you are close to civilization.

Fishing is still pretty good, and the parties from the various camps do not do much fishing. In spite of its size, the lake is not deep. If the lake was subjected to the fishing pressure of some of the more accessible lakes it would soon be spoiled.

When it was called White Trout, the long arm that is called Grass Lake was known as Grassy Bay. The large amount of rushes and other marsh grasses that grow near where McIntosh Creek comes in was no doubt the reason for the name. On the west side of Grassy Bay the McLaughlin Brothers had their depot camp. There was and still is a very large clearing, and a number of log buildings. One of the old buildings was used as a Fire Rangers cabin after lumbering operations were finished, until the new Rangers cabin was built during the last war.

There is a high rock cliff right across the bay from the Depot, which is quite high, and I imagine everyone who passes thinks how nice the view would be from the top. The first fire tower was built there, but it was found that the view from the top was not as far reaching as was supposed and the tower was moved to its present location. Anyone who has ever done any building will look with *both* delight and dismay at the many rocks that lie at the foot of this cliff. With delight because many of them are of such a shape and size that they would make the very best quality stones for a fire place. With dismay, because it would be impossible to get them away from the lake.

When the lumber companies were operating there, the dam at the foot of the lake was kept in good shape, and as a result the lake was always high, it was good paddling up the several creeks that came into the lake. Last time I was there the dam had given out, and the water was several feet below the usual summer average. This made for poor travelling and in some cases extra carrying. I have been told the dam has since been repaired, and the water is back to its normal level.

There are some lovely sand beaches on the east side of the lake. This was a popular place to camp years ago, as there was plenty of room to walk along the beaches. It is not always nice camping where there is a lot of sand, as it does not take long for sand to get into everything. But along the beaches there is usually plenty of driftwood to be easily gathered, and the breezes keep the bugs away.

Many years ago I was one of three guides that was camped there with a large party. I was by far the youngest guide, and a day or two later another party camped nearby, and one of my best friends, an Indian boy, about my age, was one of the guides with the new party. We visited a lot, and one of the men mentioned that with so many deer around it did not seem right that we had to have a steady diet of fish. One thing led to another, and finally a bonus of $25.00 was offered for fresh meat.

The older guides of course had more sense than to think anything more about it, but this other boy and I decided we wanted that money, and killing a deer did not seem then such a terrible offense.

So we spent our spare time making a bow, and some arrows. The bow was made of ironwood, and after a day working on it over a slow fire, it had a good strong spring to it. That night the two of us paddled all the way to Grassy Bay and the Depot Camp, and it did not take much searching to find a couple of old files. We heated them and drew the temper, and with the aid of a fairly good file and the man powered grindstone we made them into two edged arrow heads. The arrows made of good selected cedar, were split and the heads inserted, and then soundly wound with fish line. Some feathers found on the beach completed the job, and we had two very lethal arrows, or so we thought.

That night we borrowed a flashlight, and started after the reward. We were both familiar with the methods used for jack lighting deer, and had prepared a birch bark hat or at least a round affair worn on the head, and we fastened the light on it. When my friend put it on his head it made a very good search light.

I did the paddling. We headed for the bay where Otter Slide Creek comes in, as there is a lot of shallow water, and we wanted to get as close as possible to a deer if we were lucky enough to see one.

There were a lot of deer in the year of 1918. Any place you looked there were deer. And on any of the larger marshes there were numbers of them. We were not long in the bay before my chum held up his hand, and then pointed. I feathered the canoe as quietly as I could, and on his next signal he held up his hand again, and as pre-arranged I waited until he had put on his headgear and adjusted the light. Moving quietly along I could soon see the deer, a small one, and it seemed to be fascinated by the light. It faced the light first, and then turned so it was almost broadside, and facing just a little away, as if to be sure of a good start if it had to run. My chum with bow was ready, and I waited but he held his arrow until we were not more than six feet from the deer. The arrow hit with a thump, and we could see it was a good hit. The deer took off on the run, but before we could get our wits straightened out we heard it floundering in the water. When we reached it, it was dead and we did the necessary butchering while it was still in the water. The arrow had entered behind the ribs, and had gone in lengthwise, penetrating several inches beyond our eight inch heads.

We caused quite a commotion when we returned with the deer. The older guides gave us a talking to, about game laws, etc., but they had not tried to stop us. I noticed the next day when they had steak that they ate as much as any of us. With more than twenty people eating the deer had no chance to spoil, and not a bit was wasted. We had steak, stews, and roasts, and it was a very agreeable change from the fish diet. Only thing, we did not wait long enough to eat it. Of course, with it being warm weather, and the chance of meeting a Ranger, we did not take any chances of things going wrong, so we ate until it was gone. The only bad results were that no one needed a laxative for several days. Oh yes, we were paid the twenty-five dollars.

Many years ago my Father had a trapping camp on the east side of White Trout. I never did get to see the spot, and it was burned by early lumbermen.

McLaughlins of course, were the big operators around Big Trout, and their operations continued long after the Park was established. I never did know who were the first lumbermen there. When my father made his first trip, which I think was in 1888, a crew was just starting to build the dam at the head of the falls where Otter Slide Creek comes into Big Trout. Neither did I ever know just how they got in or from where.

Outside of the original pine trees, long since turned into lumber, I do not think there is much difference in the general looks of the woods as it is now and as it was when my Dad saw it seventy-five years ago. I hope it can continue to look as natural to the people who come to enjoy it today.

Dixon Lake (Lake Clear)

If you were to be telling some friends or acquaintances about a fishing trip to Algonquin Park, and told them you had been at Clear Lake, very few, if any, would know where you had been. Everyone, knows now about Dixon Lake, but it was first known as Lake Clear. It is quite understandable how it first got its name, for the water in the lake is very clear. I first visited the lake briefly in 1925, but later made several trips there.

It is still one of the most beautiful lakes in Algonquin Park, but then it was even more so, when the pine trees had not been cut. There are not so many pines on the ridges around the lake, but there are enough to add beauty.

It was quite a trip to get to Dixon years ago. There were no motor boats to take the party up Opeongo, and it was quite a paddle all the way up the lake. The first two portages were not too bad, but the last one was one of the hard ones. If my memory is right, in the years from 1925 until 1932 I made twenty-four trips over that long trail. I suppose the lakes are still the same distance apart.

The first camping trip I made to the lake was not a dry one. We had spent the previous night on Opeongo, and three trips on the portages did not make for too fast time travelling. It started to rain, and then a heavy wind came up, so we had to make camp as soon as we got to the lake. The ground was, and I imagine still is, swampy, and it was hard to find a spot dry enough to stretch the tent. It was a very uninviting looking lake that afternoon, as we waited in vain for the wind to allow us to go fishing.

Next morning was better, and we started to explore the lake. We did not know the proper places to fish, but we caught one for lunch, and after that moved over to the proper camp site.

We had only a couple of days to stay, as we were on an extended tour of the

Park. We did however, find some very fine fishing. Mostly lake trout, and of a good size. I do not think we took anything under five pounds, and none larger than ten, but there were so many of them it was easy to see the lake had been only lightly fished.

This trip had been with Messrs. Folsum and Parker. Next season we went back with Mr. Folsom, his daughter Miriam, and her friend Gertrude Scott. H.H. Hines was the other guide, and this year the fishing was even better. On this trip we came the closest to being without grub than on any other. This year we had come up the lake by motor and had arranged to have a pack of supplies left at the upper end of Opeongo where the trail comes in from Crow Lake. On these long trips we were very careful with supplies, but this year it started to blow heavy gales, and we could not fish on Dixon Lake, and since we had to cross Lavielle on the way out, we had to stay at camp. That year we were on the camp site on the island, which is fine in warm weather, but when it is cold and windy there is little protection. So we were two days later leaving Dixon than we had planned, and our supplies were getting low.

Late one afternoon the wind fell quite a bit, and we decided to get across the Lavielle that evening. It was still windy, but we managed to get to the mouth of Crow River and made camp. Next day we started upstream, and that was a very fine day indeed. It was still windy, but it did not matter on the river. None of our party cared to fly fish, so Hines and I were given the rods, and after we had made our first trip over the portages, we fished back down stream. The river was not so well travelled then, and we soon caught as many trout as we could use. I believe we had fish for lunch, fish for the evening meal, and some left for breakfast.

When we got to Opeongo all of us expected to have a real good meal as rations had been short for a few days. Imagine our disappointment when we could not find our fresh supplies. I felt something was wrong, so after breakfast next morning, Hines and I started on going out by White Trout (now called Big Trout). There was not much left when breakfast was finished. Half of a fry pan cramper, no butter, small tin of bacon dripping, some tea, a bit of sugar, and some rice. There was just a small lunch for the three of them, and we hoped to be back in the afternoon, wind permitting.

We had only gone a couple of miles when we could see a motor boat coming. Getting closer, we were pleased to see that it was George Heintzman, and he had our supplies. He told us it had been too windy for the boat to make it for over a week, which we knew. So with our fresh supply of food, we continued on to complete a very pleasant canoe trip.

I was back again the next year with the same three fishermen and fisherwoman, and our guide this time was Joe Lavalee. Not the one a book was written about, but the one known as *Hay Lake Joe*, (there were three Joe Lavalee's). This time after our windy experience we decided to make another camp site. This was not much trouble, and there were plenty of spots. We picked one, cleared it, found an old camp stove, the top of which we utilized in our cooking fire place, and built a table. This year we had time to get to some of the other lakes.

We went to Little Crooked, and it was there I saw speckled trout in greater abundance than any lake I have been on. They were not large, many under ten inches, and all of them appeared to be underfed. They took almost any kind of lure. This may seem like a fish story, but I caught several with a short piece of line and a feathered hook dangling alongside the canoe.

We cut the first trail to Animous or Dog Lake that year, but did not have fishing as good as we had expected. Little Dixon was good but the best fishing was in Dixon itself. We filed the barbs on the hooks, and while it meant you lost half the fish you hooked, it was an easy matter to release fish. We did not catch many real large ones, but ten and twelve pounders were common. There were also many speckled trout that summer. Again, what I am going to relate will be hard to believe. The girls wanted to catch a real large lake trout, and we located the spot on the lake where the fishing was best. It was necessary to use about 125 feet of metal line. Now anyone who has used metal lines for lake trout knows it has to be fed out slowly. Well, this time it was not possible. In letting the line out, when it was about 60 to 75 feet out, a speckled trout would get on, and we did not want small fish, since we only kept what we could eat. Time after time when letting the line out, we would catch a speckled trout. So, this will be hard to accept, we stopped the canoe as still as possible and let the lines go straight down. This was the only way we could get the lines down deep enough for lake trout, without catching speckled.

Scotty caught our largest fish, one that weighed a bit over fourteen pounds. There was a very good picture taken and she and fish graced the new folders the Canadian National Railways issued for Highland Inn the next summer.

I had a spring trip to Dixon in 1930, which was the last time I visited the lake. Later on a Ranger's Cabin had been built there, which was much used by spring fishermen, and now I have been told, it has been torn down. Since Opeongo Lake has been in operation many fishermen have filled their creels at Dixon Lake, and I have been told that the fishing is not what it was. This is to be expected, for in spite of its surface area, Dixon is not a deep lake. But in all the lakes I have fished, whether in Algonquin Park, or in Quebec, I have never known fishing anywhere to compare with Lake Clear, as it was then when I fished with the Folsom parties in the late twenties.

Red Rock, Merchants & Happy Isle

Years ago, Merchants Lake was considered one of the very best of the fishing lakes in Algonquin Park. There seemed to be no end to the lake trout, and there were many speckled as well. When I first started to guide, it was an easy matter to catch large lake trout, and lots of them. One caught in the early 20's by a party from Northway Lodge, weighed thirty-four pounds, and is, I think, the largest officially recorded laker caught in the Park. There have been stories of trout weighing more than forty pounds, but like many such tales, most of them turn out to be slightly in excess of the actual weights.

Merchants is on the Petawawa watershed, and the creek from it empties into White Trout, or Big Trout as it is now called. Just a short portage east of Merchant is Happy Isle Lake. This lake was first known as Johnson's Lake, and as was often done then was named after the foreman of the lumber camp. The camp was once on the north side of the lake. Later I imagine, because of the colour of the water, the name became Green Lake.

In 1931 or 1932, there was a drowning accident on Happy Isle. There was a party of four camped on the island. The party consisted of a father, two sons, and a friend of one of the boys. The father, one of his sons, and the friend went fishing, and did not return. It was a very windy day and the lake known to be dangerous. All three were expert swimmers, and the mother, when first informed of the tragedy said it was not possible that they had been drowned, as they swam too well. The bodies were never recovered, and their disappearance remains one of the Park's mysteries.

When all hope of finding them was gone, the wife and mother asked permission to put a plaque in their memory, and that the name of the island be called Happy Isle, as the family had loved it so much. The Department agreed, but when the name appeared on the maps it looked like it was meant for the name of the lake, and it has been known as Happy Isle Lake ever since, one of the few name changes that I agree with.

There was almost another mystery connected with those two lakes. I believe it was 1916 or 1917, and there were two parties there, one camped on each lake. The guides were college students, as a lot of college boys guided during the summer months. I do not recall which boy visited the other, but apparently he was met by his pal in a canoe, so I presume the visitor came from Merchants, and was met by his friend who was camped on the point on Happy Isle, as it was not far from the portage. On his return, it then being late and quite dark, he somehow or other got off the trail, and did not find Merchants Lake. He tramped the woods for some time, and when he realized he was lost decided to stay put until morning. When daylight came he did not know where he was, but having some sense of direction, he started south. There are no small lakes there, as the area is on top of the divide, but he kept to his course and came out several days later, hungry but otherwise not the worse for his experience. I never did know the boy's name, but I recall the older guides wondering how a man who could not follow a good trail for three hundred yards, could find his way out across such a long stretch of country.

I never camped much on Happy Isle, as Merchants was a better spot for larger fish, and more speckled. One or two parties like the camp better on Happy Isle, and it still is a nice spot to stop.

Years ago there were only lake and speckled trout in the lake, and no one ever expected to catch bass there. Bass had worked up the river into Opeongo during the twenties, and it could only be expected that they would finally get up into Happy Isle. In the mid-thirties I was camped there with a man who liked to fly fish. As it was in mid summer the fly casting brought little or no results. One evening there appeared to be quite a lot of underwater activity on the reef just in front of the campsite. My fisherman decided to try a few casts, and to everyone's surprise caught a bass. Succeeding casts caught many bass, which we returned. The bass were all about the same size, about a pound and a half, and all were a little on the thin side. They were very hungry, as there was little in that lake to produce feed for bass. Later when telling about the catch, I found people who had caught bass there for several years.

The memory of the fishing in that lake however, is not the first thing that comes to my mind when I think of Happy Isle. I always first recall the large amounts of blueberry pie that A.E. LePage could eat.

When I started to guide, very little was known of Red Rock Lake. Maps then were not the accurate pictures they are today. I first heard of it from my Father, who had never been there, but had been told where the trail left from Green Lake. It seems that a few years before a fisherman who liked to fish new lakes hired two guides, one of them Dick Blackwell, to cut a trail to the lake, and see how the fishing was. By all reports the speckled trout fishing was what most people like to dream about. It was a well kept secret for several years, but the inevitable happened of course, and the man with a great catch finally had to tell.

The original trail left Happy Isle at the old lumber camp, and it was almost

3 miles to Red Rock. Now there are two more trails, one from Opeongo, and one from Crow River. It has been fished by countless people, and still produces a lot of fish.

Years ago there was a family from Syracuse, N.Y., who spent all summer in Algonquin Park. They camped on several lakes, changing from time to time. The family as I knew them consisted of the parents, Mr. Earl's father, a boy, Junior, two girls, Betty and Emmy Jane. They spent a few summers on Red Rock, which is not too unusual, but they did take Emmy Jane in when she was six weeks old. It did not seem to harm her, for when I saw her last she was a very healthy girl of ten.

There is a story I like to tell about a party that camped a summer on Green Lake. This was in the early thirties and since two of the guides involved are still alive, I will not mention any names. Too, some of the fishermen are still alive as well.

This particular party was one I had often guided, but that summer both my oldest brother and I were busy at Highland Inn, so we had to arrange for other guides. It was what we called a perfect party, three fishermen and three guides. The tendency nowadays is to have a guide for each two fishermen, and while it is not much extra work for the guide, it is a lot easier to please one man than two.

The party outfitted at Algonquin Hotel, at Joe Lake. As they were to be in the woods for two weeks, there was quite a bit of luggage, when everything was assembled. The youngest of the three guides complained to the chief of the party that there was too much to carry and that it would not be fair to himself and the other younger guide to have this old guide along. If I remember it correctly, the *old* guide was more than twice the age of the one who complained. The chief told him that he had been with this older guide many times, and felt that he would keep up his end, but also said that when they passed Minnesing, if it was still felt that the old guide could not do his share, they would then take another guide to help on the way in. But it was stated firmly that this old guide was going on the trip, as he was one of the very best in the Park.

That same night the young guide admitted that the older man was doing a bit more than his share and things might be alright.

The party camped at the head of Big Island or *Burnt Island*, as it is now called, and hoped to make Happy Isle in one day from there. The large amount of dunnage made it necessary for the guides to make three trips on each portage. Anyone who has gone from the head of Burnt Island to Happy Isle knows that it is a good day's work, especially with three trips on all carries.

When the party reached the campsite on Happy Isle, the two younger guides were bushed. The older man without stopping went ahead and made camp, and prepared supper. When the meal was over the chief called the young guide who had objected to taking the older man, and said, 'Well, what do you think of the old man now?' The young man admitted he was pretty good. *'Pretty good,'* said the chief, *'he is more than twice your age, he carried fifty percent more than you did all the way in, and then he had to get your supper while you slept!'*

The story has no particular moral, but I like to tell it to show that everyone is not finished when he gets past sixty.

Three guides I have known have guided until they were well past seventy. Tom Salmon, Paul Teniscoe and my Father all carried canoes and packs when they were seventy-three.

Manitou Lake (Wilkes Lake)

While most of my guiding has been in the southern section of the Park, I have had a few trips to the areas around Manitou Lake. The name changers committed their worst crime when they changed the name to Wilkes Lake. This name, unlike most of the other changes, has not been accepted, and it is still referred to in most cases, as Manitou. In this chapter we will call it by its original name.

I had heard of the lake many times. In the early days of camping and travelling in the Park, some of the more venturesome took what was called the South River trip. Parties went the usual route through the Otter Slides, White Trout, Burnt, Catfish, etc., to Cedar Lake, then northwest to Kiosk, Manitou, and Tea Lakes, and then out to South River. Later when the logging road was built, parties travelled to and from Round Lake on the log train.

The early travellers would always return with a story about the DuFond's, the Indian family who had a farm at the north end of the lake years before Algonquin Park had been established.

This family came in on an old bush road, all the way from Mattawa. They had their building and clearings near the lake, and I do not suppose that there was very much produced in the way of crops, as the soil was and still is very sandy. But they did have some horses and cattle, and cultivated some of the clearings that are still there. It must have been a lonely spot, but a more beautiful sight would be hard to imagine.

The DuFond's had a pet deer in 1912. It was not uncommon then for deer to be taken as fawns and raised as pets, though later the bucks usually got a bit cross. This deer was a male, and the summer it was a year old it had antlers with three prongs on each side. This was probably due to the fact that it had plenty of salt, as this is supposed to make antlers grow.

Many stories were told about Mrs. DuFond, better known as Suzanne. It must be remembered that the Indian women were taught to do many things that would not seem right to-day. Perhaps the men of the Indian tribes had something that we white men have not yet acquired, for they taught their women to do most of the work, and then saw that they did it. Too, reports from men who were amongst the Indians years ago, show that the women were content and happy with their lot.

During the first years I was in the Park, the Rangers at Manitou were Jim Sawyer, and Tom Watty. Their headquarters camp was on Tea Lake, but there was a well kept shelter hut on an island in Manitou. I could not understand why a camp would be built on an island, as there would be times in the spring and fall when it could not be reached. Later a Fire Ranger's cabin was built high off the water in a beautiful pine grove.

There does not appear to have been any drowning accidents on Manitou as there are no graves, but there is a grave on the waters edge at Kiosk, that of a young Irish immigrant, who lost his life while on a log drive.

There was, and still is good fishing in Manitou. Trouble is that the fish are not as tasty as we who are used to the fish in the cold water lakes, like to eat. Many arguments have developed over the eating qualities of lake trout, but they still are fresh trout and it would take a long time to starve eating them.

Not too far from Manitou is Three Mile Lake. The lake got its name from the length of the portage to it from Manitou. This lake when I was there some years ago was teeming with fish, both lake and speckled trout. An old ranger told me that once it had been nearly all speckeld trout, but when we were there we caught a lot of lake trout as well. Since fishermen are not allowed to fly to inland lakes any more, I imagine that this lake will perhaps be the last really good fishing lake as time goes on. That three mile carry will save a lot of fish, and it is fitting that those few who are willing to work should find good fishing at the end of the trail.

Tea lake flows into Manitou at the southern end. The portage is not long, and there has been many speckled trout caught at the pool at the foot of the chute*. The Ranger's cabin is near the outlet on Tea Lake. A very poor spot from a beauty standpoint, but a nice cabin. Anyone who admires good axe work should examine this cabin for the hewing and fitting on the corners was most decidedly done by a man who liked his work and was an expert.

There are several lakes near Tea. One of these, Lost Dog, has produced a lot of fish, both speckled and lake trout. These fish are different from the lake trout in Manitou and Tea Lakes, as they are more like the fish in the southern sections, and by their appearance must feed chiefly on plankton*. At any rate they are a lot better eating than the lake trout in Manitou and Tea. The two

---

*chute — long trough of logs or lumber to shoot timber down off hills or ravines by gravity or water power
*plankton — marine animal and plant organisms

other lakes, further on than Lost Dog, are also good, and portages should help keep good fishing there too.

Further south and east is Cochrane, once called Long Lake (now Biggar). This lake also has or had a nice shelter hut, but even when we were there in 1935 it was showing signs of disuse.

The whole section must have been very beautiful years ago. When I saw it the lumbering had finished around Tea and Manitou, and the skid ways*, old roads and abandoned camps do not make a pretty picture. Of course logs have to get out, and many men have jobs doing so, but it does seem too bad there has to be so many scars left. Logs were then being drawn on sleighs, and drawn by trucks. I have never seen the trains of logs, but have been told that there would be as many as ten sleighs to a train. These required good roads. One such road went right up through the old Indian farm, changing an attractive old clearing into a very unpleasant looking sandy ditch.

One can hardly help but compare the modern methods with the old, especially when viewing some of the unnecessary scars. When roads were cut with axes, and transporting power was horses, few scars if any were left. Old draw roads always on low land, grew over in a few years. Old camps took time to decay and disappear, but the loggers in the days of other years did not leave the hideous scars in the woods as modern operations make almost necessary.

There are not, and lets hope never will be many cottages on Manitou. I believe there are not more than two or three at the north end. I helped build the Findlay cottage, away back in 1948. The weather was very good, and it was enjoyable to be on such a nice lake. While I still think Butt or preferably Eagle Lake is the prettiest not only in the Park, but in Ontario, nevertheless it is easy to understand why the Indians called that body of water *Manitou Lake* *.

---

*skid ways — logs piled beside the main haul road during the cutting season to await the winter sleigh haul
*Manitou — Indian name for God or Great Spirit

Lake Travers

The first few years that I was in Algonquin Park, very little was generally known of the area referred to as the *North Side*. The new railroad had just started operating, and that section was quite a distance away for a canoe trip. It was 1920 when I heard about Lake Travers, and a party came back to the hotel with some Muskelunge they had caught there. No one seemed to know that there were muskies in the lake, and while it was some distance away there were quite a few parties who went there in hopes of catching a big muskie. One party from Cincinatti I believe, name of Houston, made trips there each year, and their guide, Billy Teniscoe, was one of my best friends, and I always got a first hand account of their trip.

During the summer of 1923 this party was there, and when they returned there was the usual story of the big one that got away. It seems they were fishing with linen line, and casting rods. The lure was a large Archer spinner, and for bait they had put on a sucker minnow about ten inches long. After hooking this fish it fought for an hour, and the line finally parted, and exit the big fish.

There was a large party of us camped on the lake early in August the same year, and on walking along the sandy beaches, we found a huge fish that was dead, lying at the water's edge. Closer examination showed a large Archer spinner well down in its throat, and it was indeed the fish Mr. Houston had lost. There were several guesses made about its weight. I had not then seen many muskies, but judging by the size of some I have seen mounted this fish weighed over fifty pounds.

Travers is a lovely lake. Apparently the area around had been burned some years ago, as the trees are all second growth pine, white, red and jack pine.

There is a beach on at least half the lake, and as the lake is shallow the beaches are wadable for good distances.

During the period I am writing about there were a lot of muskies in the lake, also some pickerel, and a great many bass. Channel catfish came up the river that far, and it was a lot of fun building a fire on the beach at night, then having some baited lines in the water. The catfish were not large, though we did take one that weighed fourteen pounds.

The party we were with when we found the big fish had planned on going down the river to Pembroke, but Booth's log drive had only gone as far as Lake Travers, and had been left to be completed the following year. That meant we did not get to the lower end of the lake. In Booth's time these logs had come from the upper reaches of the Pine or Tim River, and it was a two year drive to get them to Ottawa. It was not so much the time element that made the drive last two years, but that the water was usually used up by mid-July. With the low water, logs would get into shallow water, and it was slow and tedious work to keep the logs moving.

Near the foot of the falls where the river empties into Lake Travers, there is a graveyard, or perhaps a burial ground would be a better name for it. During the many years logs had been driven down the Petawawa, many of the river drivers had been drowned when jams broke suddenly, or a misstep caused a fall into fastwater. Since it was then a long way from any habitation, the only feasible thing to do was bury the unfortunate driver close by. Indeed, from Burnt, (now called Portal) all the way down, there are graves at the foot of many of the falls and chutes.

There is a similar burial ground at Radiant. I was just there on one occasion, while cruising the old McLaughlin* limits, and as there were a couple of hours to spare we looked around the old depot buildings. One could not help but marvel at the quality of axemanship shown in the hewing of the logs, and the cornering of the buildings. It had been a large depot years before, when the road came in from Deux Riviere.

Off to one side, and in a lovely setting of pine trees there is this little graveyard. There is a plaque, and I am sorry I did not get the inscription on it, but some family who lost a son in the First War had taken it unto themselves to keep the little graveyard clean and tidy, in memory of their son.

But to get back to Lake Travers, this burial spot was picked first because it was handy, and again because the digging was easy. When we were there one spring, the driving crew had stretched their tents right on the same spot. Invited into the cook tent for a cup of tea, it seemed just a bit odd that the cook had his cot across two of the graves. I don't think he believed in ghosts.

Tom McCormick told a group of us an amusing story once about a drive he had been on years ago. Not a big crew, and the cook did not have a stove, and all cooking was done by an open fire. Bread and beans were baked in the sand,

---

*McLaughlin — McLaughlin Bros. of Arnprior, pioneer lumbermen

and all other baking was done with a reflector. Appears that it had been raining for several days and never got dry enough for the cook to make a sand hole, and not until the gang reached Travers was there sand and weather suitable. First night there he prepared his fire, and did manage to bake bread, and later put two large kettles of beans in for the night. This is by far the best way to prepare beans, and they are hot for breakfast. Well, further up the river there was trouble and quite a jam of logs piled up, so the dam at Cedar Lake was opened, and left running too long, and the flood reached Travers during the night, and tents that were stretched close to shore had to be abandoned. No serious damage was done, but according to Tom it was rather an unusual sight to see the cook out in a boat the next morning hunting for his bean pots.

It was an easy matter to catch bass the year we were held up by the log boom in the lake. The fishermen were not too ardent, and as the weather was warm and sunny we did not do much fishing until late in the day. As the waters in the lake were not deep, the bass were not the best eating, but there were a great number of them.

Not many years after we had spent such a nice time there, a hotel was built, I believe right where we had had the camp site, and a nicer setting could not be imagined. However, with the heavy fishing that resulted, the muskie and bass fishing did not last too long, and I think the camp as a hotel had been discontinued.

But it is not the fishing and scenery at Lake Travers that I will remember the longest. From the railroad station into the lake is a distance of perhaps two miles, through a nice pine forest, even if the pines are on the small side. It may not be the same now, but years ago, early in the spring, the Arbutus grew perhaps more abundant than in any other spot I know. There were several places that you could catch fragrance just walking along the road.

I was never lucky enough to help in catching a really large muskie. My best to date was in 1925 with Mr. Folsom. We were camped at the railroad, and just went in for the day. Part way we discovered the net had been left at camp, which is not too unusual on a fishing trip. We caught a few bass, trolling with spinners, and finally hooked a muskie that weighed between nine and ten pounds. Then passing a weed bed something hit the line and Mr. Folsom said he was caught on weeds. Just as I had the canoe almost stopped to turn around a fish came out of the water in a fine leap, and for half an hour we had a lovely contest with a very nice muskie. When it finally tired we did not know just how to get it in the boat. After some discussion we decided to beach it, and picked a nice clean spot close by. By the time we got out of the canoe the fish had revived somewhat, and put on another show for us. By the time he had quieted again I had cut a small pole with a crotch on it which I managed to hook in his gills, and we pulled the fish up on the beach. It weighed sixteen pounds and while that is mediocre for muskies, no one ever had a greater thrill than we had landing a fish without a net. It is a simple matter to put your fingers in the gills of a lake trout when it is exhausted, but not a safe thing to do with *muskelunge.*

The Bonnechere Lakes

When Algonquin Park was first established, the Bonnechere Lakes were not then included. The extra territory was added about 1912. These lakes, of which there are four, are connected and flow to the creek that drains Cache Lake, and are part of the Madawaska Rivershed.

The lakes are beautiful. Not very large, and there is no danger of high winds preventing fishing. The lakes have not always been considered good fishing lakes. Many years ago the area was trapped by men from the Haliburton area. They did not know that the lakes contained fish. One old trapper I talked to told me that they went all the way to Smoke Lake to fish, and that meant they went through the Bonnechere, Black Bear, Porcupine and Ragged Lakes, all good fishing lakes, to catch fish in Smoke Lake.

There is also Cradle Lake, not a very large one, but it contains, or did, a lot of fish, and they are of the plankton eating variety, and these make the best eating.

There was lumbering in the early days, and there are many places where one can see the remains of old camps and in some places only the foundations are left. The lumbering was all for pine, and by the looks of the camps there were two periods of cutting, so perhaps they cut square timber first.

As logs were driven down stream in those days, the early lumberman made use of all the streams they could. Many of the streams connecting lakes could not be used on account of their sharp drop, or small size. It was a common thing to build flumes* from one lake to the next which were controlled at the top with a dam. When water was turned into these flumes or slides, logs were then transferred down these slides to the next lake.

*flumes — wooden troughs for sluicing logs down hills

One of these was on the last Bonnechere Lake, and it went all the way to Crooked Lake. I imagine there are not too many signs of the timber used for this project, but it is all along the portage between the two lakes. Another, and perhaps longer and steeper slide went from Porcupine Lake to Ragged Lake. This slide was still in good shape when I first saw it, and it was quite a common thing for some of the younger people to walk down or up the slide in preference to the portage trail. Older and wiser people walked the trail, and did not suffer the many falls that occurred on the slide, especially if it was a bit slippery.

There is a sad note connected with the Porcupine slide, for a river driver fell into it about half way down, and was swept to his death. The last time I was there, there was not enough water in the creek to float a half loaded canoe. Looking at the remains of the slide, and almost nonexistent creek, it was hard to visualize the flume full of water and logs, and a man going to his death.

I never heard of speckled trout being caught in the Bonnechere Lakes though there should be, as there are specks in other lakes on that watershed. One thing that I never did understand is why the fish seem to avoid some of the lakes, while being plentiful in others.

On the west side there is Black Bear Lake, and then Porcupine, both well known as speckled trout lakes. These of course, have no connection with the lakes on the east side of the watershed.

Southeast from Crooked Lake and two portages away is Lake Louise. Even before I had made a trip there I had heard of the steep hill as the first of the portages leave Crooked Lake. There may be others, but as far as I know, this is the steepest trail in Algonquin Park.

There is a lake south of Louise called Welcome Lake, and it empties into Penn Lake. Years ago, Tom McCormick had some speckled trout fingerlings planted there, then it seems they were forgotten. Years later someone discovered there were fish there, and many in excess of six pounds were taken. Some of these have been on display at the Sportsmen's Show in Toronto, and they are magnificent specimens.

About 1920, George Stringer, cut a trail into Grace Lake, and found that the lake seemed to be full of large speckled trout. There were many fine catches taken here and for a few years it looked like the supply was endless. Inevitably the pressure took effect, and as it is a small lake the fishing when it got down did not quickly come back. One of the largest speckled trout I have heard of being caught, was from this lake several years after it was considered just another lake. It was not weighed, but the lucky party brought out a picture and the measurements, and it must have been well over seven pounds.

West of Bluff Lake is McGarvy. I think there is another name for it now, but it wad McGarvy years ago. The southern boundary of the Park cuts this lake.

There used to be a lot of fish in McGarvy. It was always easy to catch what was needed, but it was too far from the Hotels to take any home. I was there during the last war. I had done a bit of bragging to the men I was guiding, about the large speckled trout we would take in Grace Lake, and the large lakers we would catch in Bluff Lake. But if we had not carried a few from Louise to eat, we would have gone hungry, for we drew blanks on each lake.

Fortunately, the fish were biting like mad in McGarvy. Photos of mine show that we were using William's Wobblers, and in those days, we did not need or use a bit of minnow for added attraction. I do not remember how deep we were fishing, but it was late in the season and we did not fish deep. I do know that in less than an hour and a half we caught ten fish, and they ranged from five to eight pounds, one of the nicest catches of lake trout that I have helped to catch. We left the lake at four-thirty, and by way of Coon, Porcupine and Smoke, returned to Highland Inn late that evening.

Opeongo Lake

The first years I guided in Algonquin Park, Opeongo Lake did not have the popularity that it achieved later. For one reason, it was some distance away, and then the fishing was for trout only. But lake trout fishing was fabulous. There seemed to be no end of the good sized lake trout that could be caught. Notwithstanding the fact, that netting on a large scale had been permitted during the last year of the First War, fish could be caught almost anywhere. I talked to one of the men who had assisted in the netting and they had taken out many loads of large lake trout.

This netting did not appear to affect the fishing. It was still an easy matter to get the limit, and also easy to catch fish of ten pounds or better.

Years before the Whitney Lumber Company had built a log road and logs from Opeongo Lake were taken by rail to the mill at Whitney. When the limit had been cut off, the road was abandoned and the steel was lifted to be used on another railroad line. The old road bed was then made into a wagon road which is still in use, though the road today bears only a faint resemblance to the trail we travelled on just after the First War. It was quite an event when Sandy Heggart purchased a Model A Ford and with some slight improvement to the other road transported passengers in and out of that section of Algonquin Park. If my memory serves me correctly, the Ford made its appearance about 1924.

Bass made their appearance in the mid-twenties, having worked their way up the river from MacDougalls (now called Booth) Lake. The presence of bass of course meant less feed for the lake trout, and with the heavy fishing which always follows accessibility, the fishing in the lake has tapered off. There is still good fishing but it's difficult to compare with the kind of fishing we enjoyed over forty years ago.

The first time I saw Opeongo Lake was on my first trip as a guide, in August of 1917. We had left Merchants Lake early in the morning, and in spite of making three trips on the portages we arrived at Opeongo in the early afternoon. The lake was calm, and the older guides decided that it would be better to camp at the dam at the outlet, in case it was windy the next day. At that time, there was a clearing and some old buildings on the south side of the channel, just east of Sunnyside. These had belonged to some of the Dennison family, who had the farm where the large clearing and buildings stood on the east side of the next bay.

At the head of the lake we had been told by Fred May, one of the older guides, about a man who had been killed by a bear while the bear was caught in a trap. It seems that the senior Dennsion had paddled with his grandson Hal, a boy of nine, (who was later accidentally shot at Annies Bay, while attempting to remove a rifle from a hand sleigh). The trap was set not far from water, and it appeared a bear had put his foot in the trap, and taken the trap and dragged it away in the woods. Just a short distance in the woods, the trapper stepped over a log and right onto the bear who was still in the trap. The trapper it seems, knew he was doomed, and called to the boy to go for help. By all accounts the boy of nine paddled back to the farm six or seven miles, for help. The father of the boy, and a man named Finlayson, went back, but the old man was dead when they arrived. He is buried at the Dennison farm, and I believe it is still possible to locate the grave.

In the next few years I asked many questions about the tragedy. All the old timers knew of it of course, but no two stories were exactly alike. I got to know Mort Finlayson pretty well, as he fire ranged for years afterwards, and I had been guiding. He did not appear to want to talk about the bear incident. In the winter of 1918 I met a Mr. Dennison at a lumber camp and when I introduced myself we had a nice talk of early times. My grandfather and he had been very good friends. After a few very pleasant evenings, I asked about his father and the story of the bear. From what he would tell me, I got to know not a bit more than I had from all the stories I had listened to. I am perhaps the last person living who talked to both Mort Finlayson and Hal Dennison about the bear that supposedly killed the senior Dennison, and I did not learn a thing. Some years later I was told that circumstances of his death were not just as everyone had been led to believe.

Mr. Dennison, who was then a man in his seventies, told me many fishing stories. I asked about large fish, and he told me that the largest fish he had caught, was taken in what he called Johnsons Lake (Happy Isle Lake). Just why he would leave Opeongo Lake, with the choicest of fishing, walk the several miles to Johnsons Lake and take the trouble to set a net under the ice I can't understand.

Their only scales were a set of beam scales, used for weighing quite large bundles or objects, but he was quite emphatic in insisting that this large lake trout weighed almost sixty pounds. There is no official record of course, as this was seventy-five years ago or more, and most of the fish caught in that lake are in the usual two pound or even smaller class. I have known of quite a number that were in the larger than average class, but never one like the one he described.

Opeongo is quite the largest lake in Algonquin Park, and has some lovely scenery, and fine beaches. When the depths of the lakes were taken some years ago it was found that in spite of its size Opeongo was not a very deep lake. By all accounts it received its name from Chief Opeongo, one of the famous Algonquin Chiefs, who, tradition had it, is buried on the large island. Loggers have told me that in cutting pine on the islands, many Indian graves were disturbed. With the abundance of fish, and the many lovely camping spots, it is easy to believe that Indians would want to live on such a beautiful lake.

As a very inquisitive boy of eighteen you can imagine that I asked Mr. Dennison many questions about game, especially wolves, deer and beaver. He told me that there had been deer, but they were quite scarce about the time the Park was established. There were wolves, but he did not recall them being very plentiful. Beaver were very scarce, there was plenty of mink, marten and fisher, with a few otter, although not the quantities that there are today.

During the twenties the rules regarding crown leases were relaxed, and several leases were granted on the lake. The rule permitting leases was recinded the next year, but the leases already granted were permitted and as a result there are some cottages on Sproule Bay.

Sandy Heggart obtained a lease near where the road hits the lake, and on the spot where the lumbering buildings had stood. He built some cottages, but later sold them to Joe Avery, who conducted a resort and outfitting store for several years until his death. There is a good road, and many people get to see the lake during the course of the summer.

Some years ago, when the first studies were being made of the local fishing, a laboratory was built at Opeongo. This project under the supervision of Dr. Harkness, who later became the Chief of the Division of Fish and Wildlife at Queen's Park. The Lab was named after him, and dedicated to his memory following his death.

Lake Louise

Lake Louise is one of the most beautiful lakes in Algonquin Park. It is not on any large water chain as it sits near the top of the divide, and its waters empty into Rock Lake, which, as everyone knows, is part of the Madawaska River chain. It is fed by only a few small unimportant lakes.

No one seems to know for certain where the name came from, but some of the old people I talked to half a century ago told me one of the early trappers named it after one of the women in his family. It really does not matter, but it is nice that when the name changers made such a mess of the lakes, they left Louise as it was.

I have not been there for many years, but it was always known as a lake well supplied with lake trout. These were small, but extremely good eating and no end to the supply.

There should be some bass in Louise as well. In the summer of 1923 I was there with a small party, and we were camped near the western end of the lake. One morning I noticed a bunch of fish nearby, and was amazed to see they were bass, some of them a good size. I got a line and managed to catch one, which we did not need or keep, but I never heard of others being caught. No doubt by now someone else has found them, as it would not be impossible for them to come up the creek from Rock Lake. In the more than twenty years I guided from Highland Inn, I heard of only one speckled trout being caught there, and that was taken by the late Dr. Devitt of Bowmanville, one of the all-time well-known summer visitors to Algonquin Park.

It is odd there is not a quantity of speckled trout in many of the lakes of the Madawaska chain. There were several lakes that were well known for specks, but others did not appear to have them. The first years that I was at the Inn, it was no bother to get a mess of speckled trout in Little Island Lake, just about the head of the chain. Source Lake, a beautifully clear lake, did not have them and Source Lake, formerly called Caroline Lake, is the top lake on the Madawaska River. Iris Lake, which is also a small lake at the head of a creek, part of the Madawaska chain, has speckled trout, and Kathleen Lake, now closed to fishing, has produced many speckled, some of them a good size.

Lake Louise was not included in the original tract set aside for Algonquin Park. The former boundary crossed the south end of Harness Lake, and because of that, the original name was Boundary Lake. The area containing Louise, Crooked and the Bonnecherre group was taken into the Park in 1912.

The Sawyer family, trapped that area about a century ago. About 1890, they sold their interest to my grandfather and my father, and they trapped there for a number of years. I never did get there with my father to be shown just where their camp had been, but it must have been a wonderful place. No one went far from a canoe route in those days and their route would go along the now regular trails to Black Bear, south to Coon and McGarvy, and back to Louise.

Years ago there were buildings at the eastern end of the lake, and the portage to Rock Lake had been a wagon road, no doubt used for toting supplies in to the camps. They must have had a boat and crib* on the lake to move supplies to the western end, as there are or were signs of wagons being used along other portages. It is odd how wagon tracks remain long after most other signs have been erased or covered.

The original shelter hut was part way down the lake on the south side, on a very nice point with pine trees and a view both ways on the lake. Later a cabin was built near the portage going to the lake we knew as Rough Lake. There was also the old camp down the western bay, years ago known as Thompson Bay. This was so called because the camp had been built and used by Matt Thompson. Matt Thompson had killed a man in a fist fight, and I have never been able to find out if he stayed there when he was in hiding, or after he had served a term in the penitentiary. The camp was almost a dugout, built like a T and hardly big enough to move around in.

There are two lakes south of Louise that should be mentioned. They do not connect with Louise, as they are on the other side of the watershed, but years ago both were known as good fishing lakes. The first one, perhaps two miles from Louise, was known years ago as Rough Lake, because of its tendency to be very rough when windy. Just a short distance south of this lake is another smaller lake, originally named Gull Lake, but now called Grace Lake.

Rough Lake as we will call it, has, or did have, some good-sized trout. We fished it quite a lot with the Davis party in the early thirties, and caught many in the ten pound class. There were speckled trout too, and good-sized ones, though we never took one larger than five pounds. Grace Lake however, has or had then produced many large speckled trout. There was one very large

---

*crib — 20 pieces of square timber locked between two big logs which served as a floating raft

fish taken there years after and it was considered over the hill. I did not see the fish, but the party brought back pictures and measurements. I do not recall the exact measurements, but there is a rule that is more accurate than most scales. That is by squaring the girth, multiplying that sum by the length, and dividing the result by 800*. The answer is very close to the actual weight of the fish, and after computing the figures they gave us, the fish weighed over seven pounds. The pictures they had, upheld our figures, and it is too bad they did not get it mounted.

Just a passing mention of McGarvey Lake. This lake was not all in the Park when I was there and it was then just becoming known as a good lake for trout. The two lakes I have been writing about drain into that lake and from there on into other lakes and eventually into Hollow Lake. I have been there several times and we only caught what fish we could eat. During the early part of the last War I was there on a quick trip and we stopped there for fish to take back to the hotel, and eventually home. I think this was perhaps the best trout fishing I ever had in the southern section of the Park, beaten only perhaps by the fishing in Dixon, when Dixon was known as Lake Clear.

We had only one copper line, so the men took turns fishing. We were just fifty-five minutes getting ten lake trout and the fish were all in the seven or eight pound class. The next morning at Highland Inn, cleaned of course, and sixteen hours out of water, they weighed a total of fifty-eight pounds.

---

*$Girth^2$ x length — 800 = lbs.

Rainy Lake (Rain)
Part 1

I tried once to find out who had given this lake the name '*Rainy*'. Any people I asked simply knew it as Rainy Lake. That was the name it carried when the railroad came through in the mid-nineties.

In the summer of 1918, I was on a train going into Algonquin Park and got talking to an old man who turned out to be Jim Sawyer. I knew he had trapped around Rainy Lake, so I asked him where the name came from. As far as he knew, Jake Clancy, the first recorded white person to trap there, called it Rainy Lake because he encountered so much rain when he was on that lake. The name stuck for a number of years after the railroad began operations.

As most people know, there is another Rainy Lake away out in Western Ontario. So many parcels and mail arrived at the wrong Rainy Lake, consequently the name was changed. Not the name of the lake, but the railway station that had been Rainy Lake Station was changed to McCraney. To add to the confusion the post office, also called Rainy Lake, was changed to Brennan. The local people did not take kindly to the name changes.

Rainy Lake in time became Rain Lake, when so many of the names of other lakes were changed. To many it just looked like someone sitting in an office miles away wanted to make a few changes. One thing, it did not spoil the beauty of Rainy Lake, but coming generations will just know it as Rain Lake.

The Brennan Lumber Company moved their mill to the lake not long after the railroad came through. I cannot find any records of any lumber company operating in the district previous to the railroads arrival. There was a square timber camp in McCraney, not too far from Round Lake and another camp at Snowshoe, both before the advent of trains. The logs and timbers had to be taken down the river to Huntsville.

I believe Brennan's Mill was or had been somewhere near Novar. As is usual, when the pine was finished, the mill had to be moved to where there was more timber. It must have been late in the nineties when the mill was taken to Rain Lake, as the community was well established by the turn of the century. A Toronto lady, Edith Chapple, taught at Rain Lake near the turn of the century and it was her first school. The school, doubled as a church, and Rainy Lake had its own Orange Lodge, which affiliated with the Orange Lodge in Kearney after the mill had been moved, this time to Kearney.

The mill, when in operation at Rainy Lake, was one of the most modern of its kind. It had a double cut band saw which meant a much larger cut could be made than from mills still using circular saws.

The foremen in the lumber camp Robert Anderson, and Dave Wilson, were considered at that time to be about the best camp foremen to be found. Both men have small lakes named after them. Wilson Lake, only a short distance from Rain Lake, and two lakes in Butt that drain into Magnetwan Lake called Anderson Lakes. Both men were in charge of camps on these lakes.

When the mill first was operating in Kearney the foreman was 'Bisco Bill' Armstrong. He was given that nick-name earlier at the mill in Biscotasing. Later on, Dave Sword from near Parry Sound was the "walking boss".

There is a story about one of the men who worked in the camp when it was at Casey Lake. A telegram had come to a man named Wm. Erwin, whom I worked with in the mill at Kearney, in 1912 and 1913, telling him that his wife was very ill and he should come home. No effort was made to take the message to him and only when he came in from a day in the woods did he get it. He did not wait for supper, but hurried to catch the passenger train which would be at the station about six-thirty. He had about five miles to walk and was about two hundred yards from the station when the train left. Undaunted, he struck out for Scotia Junction, another twenty-three miles. Again, he just managed to make the eastern platform to see the midnight train pull out. A sympathetic operator arranged for a ride to Huntsville on a freight, but his wife had passed on when he arrived at his own house.

Brennans drew logs and square timber all the way from Eagle Lake (now called Butt) to Rainy Lake.

Huntsville Lumber Company had headquarters at Rainy Lake, and they cut timber, all pine, by the waters that flowed into the Big East River. When I first trapped in McCraney there were many camps still standing that they had used. As late as the mid-forties, I used lumber from one to build a line camp. These logs were driven to their mill at Huntsville.

The J.R. Booth Lumber Company also had headquarters at Rainy Lake. There were two white frame buildings on the point across from Brennan's Mill, in fact, right where the Ranger Cabin is now. There was a good log stable at the edge of the woods. Booths used this as a sort of depot, and had a tote road* all the way to the Little Nippissing River. They must have been just cutting square timber then, for the logging was done in my time.

By such a road, I was asked to go to Eagle Lake once, with a message to the

Ranger, who happened to be my dad. I do not recall the message, but it was just about the time of year when the ice was going. The snow was already gone, but there was still ice in good condition. This was on May 3rd, and I remember when I got to the camp on Eagle that Dad had told me he had crossed the lake that morning, but would not try again.

Chester McConkey had a contract to take out cordwood near the end of the First War, and some of the wood-cutters lived in two houses at Eagle. Quite a few of us from Kearney worked there when the wood was being loaded, and the old Brennan's boarding house was used as a camp.

About 1906 Brennans took out a cut of hardwood. Many of the logs sank right at the end of the lake, and after the road was in operation Bill Fetterly from Kearney took out the many logs he raised from the bottom of the lake.

There had been two drownings in Rain Lake. The first when an overloaded boat capsized, and the only swimmer of the four decided to swim to shore and did not make it. The ones who clung to the boat were saved. More recently a fisherman stood up in a canoe, not far from shore, and lost his balance. He too, was a swimmer, but something must have gone wrong, as he did not make it to shore.

---

tote — a bush trail used for portaging supplies to camp

Rainy Lake (Rain) Part 2

Two other lumber companies in more recent years have operated at Rain Lake, or as the station was called, McCraney.

Canadian Wood Products obtained permission to cut veneer birch on part of the Brennan limit in the Fall of 1936. Then a few years later another company took out logs and cut them in a small mill that sat just about where the Brennan mill was standing. In the late twenties Chester McConkey took out the logs from the lots north of the R.R., and inside the Park, but these logs were shipped out by train.

Just about the close of the Second World War, Muskoka Wood built a set of camps at the gravel pit and for a number of years shipped logs to their mill at Brule Lake. Then Peter Thompson, who had a mill in Kearney, used the same camps and the same siding to take their logs to Kearney. They had cutting rights around Moose (McCraney) Lake. The logs from Thompson's operation were the last logs to be transported on the railroad.

When the railroad was carrying wheat from Depot Harbour to Montreal it was a very busy line. McCraney was considered about central between Depot harbour and Madawaska. There was an operator during the night hours, and an agent during the days. As far back as anyone can tell me, Jack Smith was the agent. I do not know the year he came but he only left after the wheat started to be shipped down through Washago, and most of the smaller stations on this line were abandoned.

Besides having 24-hour service at the station, there was a water tank and coal shoot at McCraney. The coal shoot was not in use that last year the R.R. ran trains, but the water tank was kept busy. They were dismantled when the road closed, though the station had been torn down before that.

There was a gravel pit about half-way down the lake. The long fill on the

R.R. was once a timbered bridge, and the gravel to fill in that bridge came from this pit. One of the section men who worked there years ago, told me that somehow or other the bridge caught fire and was weakened enough that it was not safe for a train to cross. Passengers were transferred by boat and canoe. Then after a lot of work the two sidings were joined and the trains managed to slowly go around the bridge. The trouble was the long passenger cars would hardly turn the curve. Seems odd to have taken so much time and money to build a long bridge when they had only sand and gravel to move over one very small creek.

I worked one Fall with Frank Brushey. He had worked on the section many years, along with his brother. Once, when the Brushey's were at McCraney after school had closed, the local women decided they should have a bit of a holiday. Most had relatives fairly close and of course they travelled by train. So, the men, I believe there were five, decided they as well should do something to relieve the monotony of a six-day work week. They put their hand car, (no gas cars then), on the evening express and unloaded it at Kearney. There were two licensed hotels then, and they had a good evening by all accounts. They pumped the hand car all the way back to McCraney and watched for trains. Since they were going to be alone all week, they decided they should have a case of whiskey, which I was told held 24 bottles. They got home without any trouble, put the hand car away, and before they went to bed decided they should have another drink. They did and the five of them emptied a bottle. Then someone suggested they should hide the rest of the case, as they no doubt would sleep in, and if the men from the mill came around they might lose their week's supply. So they hid the remaining 23 bottles, then took off to bed.

Early in the morning, before daylight, one of the men wakened feeling terrible. What is that excuse they use for another drink? Hair of the dog that bit you? Anyway he wanted a drink and all he could find was an empty box. Then he recalled they had hidden it all, and so he started to look ..... everywhere. Finally he called for help, and soon all five were looking for those 23 bottles, but had no luck. No one could remember where they had been hidden. Rather discouraged they almost gave up, thinking perhaps the mill men had been there. It was getting daylight when one of them happened to look out the window and there on a pile of ties, in plain view of any person who might pass by, were their 23 bottles of whiskey.

The first camp or cottage to do with the tourist trade was built on Rainy Lake in 1925. Charles Waterhouse, who owned Deerhurst Lodge on Peninsula Lake, wanted an outpost for some of his fishermen. He obtained a lease not far from the portage to Casey Lake. Then in 1937 Leopold MacAulay and Harry Tyres built a fine log cottage on the island. Later it was sold to the Nunn family. After them, it returned to Lands and Forests and demolished in 1966.

Many people, campers and fishermen went into the woods from Rainy Lake and Tom McCormick, then Chief Ranger, suggested a flag station. Logs were cut and peeled, two gangs of section men helped, cottagers also supplied help, and we had a nice log station called Eagle Lake Landing. This was moved when the steel was lifted.

In 1944 we obtained a lease, and eventually built three cottages. Many people have enjoyed a holiday there, and they are still in use. My son obtained a lease in the early fifties and built a cottage, but when he was in college cash got low, so he sold it. It too has been burned. The Waterhouse cottages, or camps, changed hands at least twice. When the train service deteriorated this place was also given up. Our cottages are now the only ones left on the lake. The lease will no doubt last years longer than I will.

I believe the first trains began in 1895. Then it was the Canadian Atlantic. It was taken over by the Grand Trunk about the turn of the century and as most know became the Canadian National in 1922. The rails were lifted in 1959. Many hunt camps then came in by train, so the hunters obtained permission to remove the ties and use it as a road. Later is was taken over by Lands and Forests, and now a fine gravel road goes right to the lake and is kept in good condition.

Many parties use this entry for trips into the interior of the Park. For several years there was a trailer for the gateman or ranger, but in 1976, a log building that I remember well from Cache Lake was moved and rebuilt at the end of the road. Robert (Bob) McCormick has been in charge since the road had been improved.

Rain Lake was once known for being one of the best bass lakes in the Park. Too, there was good lake trout fishing, only the section where it is deep enough for trout is small. Over the next portage is Jubilee, where the largest bass taken in Ontario came from one year. Islet and Hot Lakes produce many bass. South is McCraney Lake, first known as Moose Lake, and many trout, both lake and speckled, have been taken there.

Eagle Lake (Butt Lake)

I mentioned that I considered Eagle or Butt Lake the best of all the very fine lakes in Algonquin Park. The lake is not large as lakes go, but the largest in that area. In all, it is about four miles long, and perhaps one and one half miles wide at its widest point. This lake drains into Daisy Lake, long considered the head of the Petawawa River. Perhaps because the creek between Eagle and Daisy is not navigable.

There are only three very small lakes that drain into Eagle, as the lake is fed mainly by springs. The water is very blue, clear and cool even in the summer. There are times when it is too cool to swim in, especially when you get older. The lake is deep, at least for inland lakes. I believe the measurements showed that it was nearly 200 feet deep, but soundings taken by different parties put the deepest spots more than that. The deeper than average depths perhaps explain the reason the fishing has kept up in Eagle, when other lakes are showing the results of the heavy fishing of the past decade. There is no doubt that Eagle is showing that excessive fishing will deplete any lake. At that, it is surprising how the lake has held up with the very heavy fishing pressure it has had to withstand, since the lake has been accessible by road.

When the settlers first came to this section of Ontario, in the early nineteen eighties, a hunt camp was built on Eagle Lake. Tim Holland, one of a family of early settlers, cut a road passable for a yolk of oxen, and took lumber in, a distance of perhaps fifteen miles from the settlements at Sand Lake. This camp was about one hundred feet from the most western point on Eagle Lake, beside the portage from Big Ham now called Hambone Lake. This cabin was still standing when I made my first trip to Eagle Lake. When the Park was established, Mr. Holland sold whatever rights he had to the Department, and the camp was used as a Shelter Hut until 1908 when the cedar log hut was built by Dan Ross.

Chester McConkey, one of the few left who was born in this area, told me about a trip he made to Eagle Lake with Tim Holland. They went in with a horse and jumper. A jumper was a hand-made sleigh, and some were made small enough for one horse. The runners were natural crooks, found in the woods, and the rest was also pole construction. This had a box four feet wide, made of pine boards twelve inches wide, and was eight feet long. The object of the trip was to get a load of fish. According to Chester, they set a net near the eastern end of the lake, near what we call Gull Rock. This was through the ice, quite a common thing then. At that time, most of the fish taken were speckled trout, many of them in the four pound class. Now the fish are nearly all lake trout.

The largest speckled trout it has been my fortune to see was caught in Eagle Lake. This was many years ago, and the fish was taken in the winter. I do not remember just what month, but I will always remember taking the fish to a store to be weighed. The fish had been caught on Tuesday, the head had been removed, and it had been frozen. When the fish was weighed on Saturday evening it was almost six and one half pounds. Some people claim that by taking off the head and taking out the guts, a fish loses one third of its weight. That would make the fish if weighed when caught, over nine pounds.

Speaking of large speckled trout, one that could well be a modern record was taken very close to Algonquin Park, and near the Eagle Lake area. Hunters had a net set for lake trout, permissable then, and were surprised to catch a very large speckled trout. I talked to one of the men who had helped catch it, and he still claims it weighed twenty pounds.

Another unusual incident about speckled trout fishing happened at Eagle Lake. Before it was part of the Park, one of the old guides, who must have been young then, was at Eagle Lake in the spring while Jim Sawyer was there trapping. They fished where Lost Lake Creek comes in, and caught many speckled trout — many over four pounds. The party were medical studetns, and many years later when my Dad was there, a party came to fish, and an old Doctor told Dad about being there years before and all the fish he caught. He was one of that party but this time they caught only lake trout. Just why a lake should change from one fish to another is a problem the biologists will have to settle.

There was another trapper's cabin on Eagle Lake. Many years before the area had been set aside as a Park, at the time my Grandfather had his camp on Roseberry, Jim Sawyer had a camp on Eagle Lake, and there is still some of the camp left. It is a bit west of where the portage leaves Eagle for David Lake. When I saw the cabin first, the roof, made of cedar scoops was still in fair shape.

An oddity in Eagle Lake is the old dead head called the Post. It is obviously the top end of a pine tree sticking about ten feet out of the water, near the south shore between Daisy and Ham portages. It sits straight up, and by measurement it is over seventy feet to the bottom. By comparing it to a pine of the same height, it must be at least thirty-six inches at the base. Just how it got there no one can be certain, but it must have fallen on the ice, floated to that spot, and there also must have been a heavy stone embedded in the roots, which caused it to sink in an upright position. My friend, Chester McConkey, told me it was there when he made his trip in over seventy years ago.

The shelter hut built by Dan Ross in 1908, was replaced by one of hewed pine, only four logs high. This was built in 1917. This camp was my Father's pride, he was assisted in the building by Rangers Watt, Sawyer, Patterson and Gaites. Patterson was a broad ax man, and his work was admired by many. The cabin was burned a few years ago, as new policies did not need the cabins for travelling Rangers to stay in.

Brule Lake

When I was a small boy I knew only of Algonquin Park as a spot that must have been far away.

In 1910 my father and one of my uncles went there to guide. In the Fall of that year my Dad was taken on as a Park Ranger, and his post office address was Brule Lake. We did not follow Dad until February of the next winter and his letters came from this place called Brule Lake. So for quite a while Brule Lake seemed to us kids to be Algonquin Park. I did not get to see the place until late in the winter in 1914.

I went with Dad on a trip to Misty Lake, checked some wolf baits and returned to Kearney. I believe we were away three days. On the way in, we had a fish on McIntosh Lake. The first lake trout I caught weighed a bit over five pounds, and that is the largest fish I ever caught fishing through the ice. I also caught a ling, the first one I ever saw. Indeed, until then, I did not know such a fish existed. We fished going in, also coming back out, and I think our catch was six fish.

The next time I saw Brule Lake was when I was with a gang of men clearing the dead brush and other debris well back from the railroad. There was a quite large saw mill there at that time. Barnet Lumber Company cut pine in that area, and their mill was there. I do not remember the year it was moved, but it was during the First War. This company must have operated in the Park years before that, as the buildings and clearing on Burnt Lake (later changed to Burnt Root Lake) was known as Barnet's Depot. I do know they had a camp on the north side of McIntosh, and knew many of the men who had worked there. The logs were drawn all the way to Brule Lake.

Brule Lake is one of the highest situated lakes that drains into the Oxtongue River. There are some smaller ponds that drain into Brule, but it is the largest body of water on the highest point of the Oxtongue system. The lumber yard for both of the mills that operated there were west of the millsite, and went right to another lake called Larkwell. This lake drained north and east of Wolf, (now called Timberwolf), then into Misty and the Petawawa River system. The difference in elevation between Larkwell and Brule could only have been a very few feet, if there was any difference.

Brule flows into Potter Lake, a distance of less than half a mile. The limit line between different cutting rights is somewhere between Brule and Potter. I do not recall the name of the one company, though the name Colonial stikes a chord. Gilmours cut the pine around Potter Lake before the Park was established. I do not know which company built the dam at the foot of Brule, but since there was the remains of a sluiceway, they must have driven logs down that stretch of creek.

McIntosh lake was where most people went to fish. Years back, when the only people were trappers or the very early lumbermen, the name of the lake was Big Shoal. Anyone who has fished there will understand why. I have been told that the name of McIntosh came from a member of the Barnet family. Close to this lake was another lake, then called Wolf Lake, with plenty of lake trout. One summer I was there with a large party, and in the evening we caught several speckled trout, all in the four pound class, one a bit more than five. But I never heard of a speckled trout being caught in McIntosh. Yet both are on the Petawawa system where many speckled trout have been caught. There are two lakes between McIntosh and Brule that empty into Brule.

In 1927, Peter Duff moved his saw mill from Round Lake in McCraney Township (outside the Park) to Brule, as he had obtained the cutting rights to a good-sized block of timber. This would be mainly hardwood (birch and maple), although one year he did have a large cut of spruce. His main camp was at Brule, and later a camp south of the R.R. at Brown's Lake. Logs were drawn to Brule by horse and sleigh, at first. I think this same company was one of the first to use trucks to pull loaded sleighs.

When Duff decided that he worked long enough his operation was taken over by the Muskoka Wood Lumber Company, who increased the size of the operation and had logs hauled from Rain Lake to Brule Lake on the Train.

For some reason never explained, the mill while in operation, took fire one night and was totally destroyed. Logs were then hauled to the Huntsville Mill on the train. After the steel was lifted in 1959, logs were drawn all the way to Huntsville by truck. They utilized the old railroad bed and then Highway 60. There is still some cutting going on there, and logs are taken to the mill at Huntsville.

Near the close of the First World War there were a number of cordwood camps in the Park all along the railroad. One at Rainy, one at Islet Lake, and one at Potter Lake. Brule was missed.

West of Brule Lake is the summit. Here there is quite a grade from each side to get to the top of the divide. It was partly because of this hill that heavy train traffic on this part of the C.N.R. was discontinued. The summer we were working on the brush gang we camped west of Brule, in an old sand pit, and while it was just the beginning of the grade, trains still had trouble.

Once there was a siding at the summit where part loads could be left, but it took too long, and was used only the odd time. The summit, highest point on a railroad in Ontario, was 1407 elevation at rail level. The hill beside it was perhaps 50 feet higher.

There is a little lake right on the top of the hill. Water runs either way, or did, depending on where the beaver had their dam. Section men talked for years about the trouble they were having with these animals. One day at quiting time they tore out a small dam. Since they would have to come back in the evening to finish the job, they left their tools, shovels and picks behind. Then one man had an idea a lantern might keep the beaver away. So a lighted lantern was hung in a tree. Just before midnight they checked on the dam and, imagine their surprise, when they found that their tools had been used to repair the hole they had dug earlier. But best of all, one old beaver was holding the lantern so the others could see to do their work.

Nipissing River

Today, with all the logging roads in that area, the Nipissing River is not the far away place it seemed some fifty years ago. At that time many of the now well travelled routes were still considered in the deep woods, and it was at least two days travel from any starting point to get to the river.

My first acquaintance with the Little Nipissing River was in nineteen twenty-three. Mr. C.P. Folsom, of Dayton, Ohio, wanted to see some of the less travelled routes in the Park. So that year we went in by way of Eagle (Butt) Lake, and took our time getting over to Roseberry. From Roseberry we took the four mile Bear Portage over to Lature Creek, which empties into the River two miles above what was then called the High Dam. Counting the portages on the way in from the railroad, there was almost nine miles of portaging to get to the Nipissing River.

We spent the first night in the shelter hut that had been built a few years previous from timbers of the old logging camp operating years before. It was late when we arrived, and we lamented that we did not have a fly rod to see if we could catch a few trout for supper. While I was getting some fresh brush for the beds (in those days spring beds and mattresses were not standard equipment for shelter huts) and opening the food packs, Mr. Folsom disappeared. I imagined he had walked over the short portage just to have a look see, but in a short while he came in wearing a grin that could almost be tied behind his neck, and carrying a nice string of small speckled trout. He had used a very small set of feathered gang hooks, a short piece of linen line and for a rod a hazel bush he had cut. That was the pattern for our fishing the rest of the time we were on the river. At nearly all the dams, if it was near mealtime, we could catch enough trout for a meal with that small feathered set of hooks.

We got away early the next morning. The water was good. All the dams were holding water, and made for good paddling. McLaughlins had repaired the dams as they had taken a drive down the river the year the First War started, and at this time Booths were getting ready to use the river to get their logs out. About noon we arrived at Dougays Camps, and at this spot the creek from Gibsons Lake enters the river. It was our plan to spend a few days on Gibsons Lake, as we had been told there was good fishing. I think we were the first party to fish it, other than lumbermen.

We had a fairly easy trip to the lake, using a good wagon road all the way. This road had been built as an access for a dam to be built. The outlet of the lake at that time, had not been flooded.

We established a camp on this very lovely lake, but we fished until dark, and again early in the morning, without getting as much as a strike. We discovered that there was not much depth to the water, as there were very few places with as much as thirty feet of water. I had been told since, that fish have been caught at that spot but you could not prove it by the fishing we did.

We did however, experience the thrill of being on a new lake, and making an original camp.

Next morning early we broke camp and headed back to the river. We arrived at the Lumber Camp about noon. To my surprise we found a group of men who were repairing parts of the river for the drive the following spring, and the man in charge was an old friend, Pete Mayhew. We were invited to have a meal with them, which was accepted perhaps more eagerly on my part than on Mr. Folsom's.

Anyone who has not eaten at a lumber camp in the 'old days' has missed an experience that can never be forgotten. In the summer of course it was not possible to have fresh meat, and most of the meat was some kind of cured pork. Camp cooks had a way of preparing even this so that it was a tasty dish. Vegetables were always well cooked, and the bread, baked at the camp, was out of this world. But the real treat were the pastries. At least two kinds of pies, two or three varieties of cake, not to mention tarts and cookies. I have eaten in many camps and the pattern was always the same. This was necessary, as the men would not stay at a camp where they did not have good meals.

To anyone who read 'Mostly in Clover', by Harry Boyle, and took an interest in the meal he described at his Aunt's, this account of mine may seem like a very weak description of a meal. But to a hungry working man, winter or summer, such a spread was indeed a banquet. I have over the years worked in lumber camps, and had such meals days on end.

The silence in a camp dining room is remarkable. Even in a small camp there is no talking at the table, but at one of the larger camps, where more than a hundred men were fed at the one sitting, it was amazing that during the whole course of the meal there would not be a sound, other than eating, or a request in a low voice for some dish to be passed.

Back in 1923, C.P. Folsom and I were told we were the first 'tourists' that the lumbermen had seen on the river. There were no travel permits then, and it is not possible to check, but I have reason to believe that we were the third party, (fishermen with guides), that had travelled the river. Two uncles of mine had taken a party down about nineteen twelve, and another party, guided by Wib Vantcleif, went down a couple of years later. The second party was trying to work their way through from Tims Lake to the South River waters, and was quite a ways down the stream before they decided they were on the wrong stream, so they just kept on going.

The day we went over to Gibson Lake we asked directions at the camp. Imagine to our surprise, late in the afternoon to have a visit from the Fire Ranger, a man named McIntyre. He told us that in three summers of fire ranging on the Nipissing River, this was the first time he had been able to report that he had travellers.

The next two days were memorable ones. There was not much portaging as the lumber dams held a good supply of water making paddling easy, and we had no schedule. This was before the pine had been cut, and anyone who has not seen a pine forest has missed a lot. There were other trees as well, but for long stretches there would only be pine. There was one stretch where the pine trees grew close to the river and their branches almost met. Any trees, large and small are nice, but it has always seemed to me that there was something especially real about pine trees. They are so large, and so noble, that when you are where there is nothing else, it almost makes you feel that you are in a church.

There were a lot of deer in those days. I forget just how many we would see in a day, perhaps fifty. There were no moose, and not as many signs of beaver as one would expect.

We reached High Falls mid-morning, and started to look for the Fire Ranger's Cabin. A brother was there, and we planned on staying that night with him. His camp was the cookery of a small camp that had been built perhaps half a mile above the Falls for the improvement crew that had been repairing the dam and log slide for the coming drives. There seemed to be no limit to the number of small trout we could catch at the foot of the Falls. These we enjoyed, as we planned on leaving the river the next day.

The portage to Robinson Lake was in a different spot then. About a mile below the Falls on the right side there is the remains of an old building that was then the Ranger's Cabin, or as they were called, a shelter hut. The portage went from there, about a mile and a half to Robinson Lake. It went through a lovely pine forest, and being almost level made a lovely walk. Not many years later when I took a party there, the pine had all been cut, and what once had been a beautiful forest was nothing more than a huge pile of slash. The location of the trail had also been changed, and it now hits the river right across from the cabin at the Falls.

We did some fishing on Whiskey Jack and Robinson Lakes. The lakes are very similar, and only a creek of a few yards separates them. In Robinson Lake we could catch only speckled trout, and in Whiskey Jack we caught only lake trout. Seemed strange, when to all appearances the lakes were identical. Just a few years ago, on my last trip down the river, we took a day and fished the two lakes. A heavy rain and thunder storm hampered our fishing, but we did catch one speckled trout in Whiskey Jack Lake.

On the way from Robinson to Burnt Lake, in one of the small ponds, we saw what I think was the largest deer I have ever seen. A deer that weighs two hundred and fifty pounds is a large deer, and I have seen less than six. But this deer, which was so big and fat it could hardly run, must have been close to four hundred pounds. There is no chance of it being a caribou for we were very close to it, and had a good look. Lovely set of antlers, still in the velvet, and a smooth sleek coat that showed it was in prime condition. The body looked almost as large as that of a cow.

We returned to Highland Inn by way of White Trout, Big Island, and Smoke Lake.

The next time I was on Nipissing, we just went to fish — the year of 1924. We camped on Robinson Lake, and walked over and fly-fished at High Falls. There was very little fishing done there then, and there was always a good mess of trout to be caught.

A similar trip in the spring of nineteen thirty-two saw a very changed picture. There was a Ranger's Cabin built on the hill at the head of the Falls, and the remains of what had been a tent camp used when another lumber company was again repairing the dams and slides to enable them to take out several cuts of pine. We camped on the lake side of the portage so we could fish up and down the river. This was in early June, and the fishing should have been at its best, but with the flood waters of the spring log drive, and the heavier than usual fishing, we did not have the luck of earlier years. There were many signs that showed that more people had found this good fishing spot. Eight years before there had not been a sign of a campsite, and one could feel truly in the untravelled woods. But now we saw signs of many parties having camped there, and it was a sad feeling to think that the last of the inaccessable spots had been opened up.

I did not see it again until 1935, when Harris Whitaker wanted to make a trip down the river. For this trip we went in by wagon to the Pine River, where the old road crossed it a bit west of the Park boundary. The trails were good then, and it was an easy matter to get from Tims Lake over to Big Windfall, which is only a short carry to the river. At this time the Paxton Dam was in good repair, and it was like travelling on a lake as far as the dam. There was a cabin in good repair close by the dam, used no doubt by the men who controlled the flood waters in the spring. Trails were not good, but were easily found and passable. The going was good, and we had no trouble making High Dam the first night on the river. We stayed in the same cabin Mr. Folsom and I had used, and while it showed signs of not being too well kept, it made a good place to spend the night. We made very good time, as Harris was a fine paddler, also much better than the average visitor on a portage. We hunted for a while to see where the portage from McLaughlin Lake came into

Nipissing, and when we did find it, I insisted that it could not possibly be in that area, and we went on. Later I found out that I had been wrong.

The dams were still holding water, but we found more lumber camps, all deserted. We spent a night in one, when we stretched a tent inside one of the larger buildings. There was just too much grass and brush outside to make a comfortable camp. We used up a bit of time the next morning collecting some of the hand-made door latches and hinges. In all we must have added twenty-five pounds to our load, which Harris carried all the rest of the trip.

The day we had spent on Windfall, the last lake before getting to the river, was not wholly of our own choosing. There had been a very heavy rain storm, and it would have been foolish to have moved on, although the extra water was good for travelling. On the reaches of the river, kept high by the old dams, it did not matter, but when we came to the parts of the river where there were rapids — the extra water saved a lot of carrying. On the longest portage on the river I suggested that Harris would walk empty, and I would try and take the loaded canoe down the rapids. This was not a very difficult feat, as there were no chutes, and no where was the water over two feet deep if one did have to get out of the canoe. The trail was about two miles and I was there waiting for some minutes before Harris arrived. When I told him how good the water was, he mentioned that it would make a nice trip, so I carried the canoe back up to the head of the rapids, and together we enjoyed a ride through the rapids.

We left the river at High Falls and made our camp on Burnt Lake, this lake being Harris's favourite of all the lakes in the Park. Later when he saw Eagle Lake, he was not so certain.

One of the evenings while camped on Burnt Lake, we went back to Robinson and Whiskey Jack for some fish. It was in the evening, and at that time of the year the blueberries were at their best. There were many patches of berries around the two lakes, and in less than an hour we had seen eight bears. We took a picture of one at less than ten feet. One very large bear was having a lunch all by himself quite close to the waters edge. We decided to try for a picture, but when we got close he took exception to either us or the canoe, and did some very angry snarling and growling. We ignored this, but as we got closer he came towards us, still not pleasant, and even waded a bit out in the water. While this was the first and only time that I had ever seen a bear show any signs of animosity, we decided we had better look for one who was on better terms with the world.

I did not see the Nipissing River again until the late fifties. My boys had made a trip in June 1950, and from their account of the trip the river had changed since I had been there. Since building cottages both at Kearney and at Rain Lake, I did not have much time for long trips, as there were always chores to do, and my guiding was confined to short trips.

By this time, I had also found that there were not many parties who wanted to go on long trips. Most people had tents and camping outfits and their idea of roughing it was to drive up to a public camp, stretch their tent, cook on a gas stove, sleep on cots or mattresses and live in close proximity with many of the same ilk. Since there are so many families doing it, they must be enjoying such a holiday. But it all seems so far removed from the idea that people had of a camping trip forty years ago. Some will say that today children of any age can enjoy a camping trip not possible any other way. Perhaps, but the Earles took a six week old baby into Red Rock Lake in nineteen eighteen, and their trip lasted almost two months.

In nineteen fifty-six I met a party from Wayne, New Jersey, who had spent several years on holidays in Algonquin Park and were looking for some different areas to travel and fish in. They were by themselves the first year, and the next summer went down the river to White Trout and back up the Petawawa. The family consisted of Jim Kelly, his wife and son Bill. They had a good time and during the trip we talked about the possibility of going down the Nipissing the following year. This was to be an extended trip, as we planned on going all the way to Brent on Cedar Lake, and then getting fresh provisions and coming back up the Petawawa to the base camp.

This time we worked our way in on an old lumber road to a lake north of Tims Lake, and planned on getting to the Nipissing at or near the Paxton Dam. We made camp along the side of the road late in the day, and early next morning started to look for the trails over to the Nipissing, but we could not locate them. There were a few spots that I could remember, and a few of the old trail blazes, but the whole area had been left in such a heap of slash following the cutting of logs that it was not possible to get a trail through.

We made a short trip down the Pine or Tim River to Roseberry Lake as we had planned. It was nice to camp on our favorite sand beach, and this time we found a good number of arrowheads and artifacts, left many years ago by the Indians who camped there.

On our return we again hunted for a trail to the Nipissing. Again no luck, and we were beginning to wonder if we would get there. Then on Sunday, a man picking berries told us he had worked in the lumber camp which was east about two miles, and that it was less than half a mile from the camp to the river. We walked to the camp, and I hunted up a trail to the river, which was easily found as there was a draw road almost the whole way. Next morning we started to carry our two canoes and camp equipment the two miles to the old lumber camp. We had one trip completed and were returning for another, when we met a small truck being driven by the manager of the Lumber Company. He loaned us the truck and the rest of the load was transported much easier than the first trip. About the time we had everything settled it started to rain heavily, and we were given permission to stay in one of the camp buildings. It rained all the rest of the day, and into the night, and we were glad to have a dry place in which to stay.

We were away early the next morning and the whole party was thrilled after the earlier disappointments to finally get on the river. Jim and the two boys got away first, and had a good look at the large cow moose feeding in the marsh.

Our entry to the river was about a mile above the Paxton Dam. It was quite different looking than when I had seen it last. The dam had rotted away, and the water was at least ten feet lower. There were hardly any signs of the cabins that had been there before. It had been pretty far gone the previous time I saw it, yet habitable; but now unless you knew where to look it was hard to find the old foundation.

From the Paxton Dam on, the river was surely wild. There had been no recent cutting, and everything looked virgin wilderness. There were many beaver dams and these helped make better paddling. We did not stop to fish, as I felt the fishing would be better further downstream. I had hoped to make the High Dam to camp that night, but late in the afternoon we quite suddenly and unexpectedly came to a bridge. It had of course been used for lumbering, but we did not know it was there, and it sort of destroyed the wild atmosphere of the river. Then on land we were more surpised to see fairly fresh tire tracks, apparently made by a small truck, and no doubt bringing people into fish. We decided to camp there that night, and the next morning continued our trip. It had been a lovely evening, and we just spread our sleeping bags for a night looking up at the stars. Nature however, decreed differently, for about three in the morning it started to rain. You can imagine the scurrying around in the dark to get the tents erected and the food packs covered.

We tried fishing at the next dam, but as the water was low we did not have any luck. In a marshy lake not far above where Lature creek enters the river, there had always been a spot, (apparently where there was a spring), that always harboured a few trout. Once there did not seem to be an end to the number of fish we could have taken. This time we did not get a bite, even with worms.

We lunched at High Dam, and the boys tried fishing without any luck. The low water was even more evident here, as the dam was not holding any water at all, and the top of the dam was at least twenty feet above the flow of the river. The old Ranger's Cabin was gone here too. Only the rusted parts of the old stove remained of what was once a very nice cabin.

The river from High Dam was very interesting, as it was quite wild, and there were a lot of deer and a few moose. We saw two bears that afternoon, the only ones we saw on the trip. Late in the afternoon we started looking for a camping spot and decided on stopping in a nice grove of pine well above the river, where we had a splendid view of perhaps four hundred acres of marsh and land that had been flooded by the next dam. It looked like a good place to see game, especially moose and deer. We did not even have the tents stretched when we saw the first deer, and a few minutes later a cow moose and her calf. Jim could not get close enough for a picture, but early next morning a small bull moose crossed, and he walked right close to it and took both movies and still pictures. When we got going again we could see that it was a regular crossing place for deer and moose, and it is probable that many crossed during the night, as well as those that we saw.

We did get enough for a meal at the next dam, and at the falls at Dougay's camp. There again we found all the camps except the Ranger's Cabin were fallen in. It seemed quite lonesome, compared to other times I had been there.

That night we camped at the next dam, the name of which I never did hear, and that was the time we got caught in a heavy rain before even one tent was stretched. Then after working and getting wet putting up the tents, the rain stopped as soon as we had shelter.

The next morning while I was breaking camp, Jim Kelly took his boy Bill back upstream to fish some of the good holes we had seen on the way down the previous day. Tod Readon fished the dam, getting many small ones, but the Kelly's came back with some very fine trout, more than we could eat in two meals.

We lunched at the lower end of the long portage, and there we saw our first and only party while we were on the river — two men. After lunch I went back and tried to bring one canoe with a light load down the same rapids I had brought Harris Whitaker down, but this time there was hardly enough water for the light canoe, and it took more time to get the canoe down the rapids than if I had carried it.

The water from there to Graham's Dam was very bad. There were a few beaver dams, and some fair paddling, but the heavy storms of a few years back, both Hazel and Audrey, had caused many trees to fall, and a number of them fell right across the river. This meant unloading the canoe and loading again, and after a few times this gets nerve-wracking, as it takes so much time. The first canoe had gone on ahead, and it was well after dark when we caught up to them. They were at Graham's Dam and it too was not holding water. To make things worse there was a portage where we used to paddle. That night it was near midnight when we had supper and got settled to sleep.

Next morning we again found another portage where there had been plenty of water, and on a hill where there had been a fine stand of pine trees was a large group of empty buildings. This had once been a lumber camp, and was later used to hold quite a number of prisoners of war, who had been sent to work in the woods.

It was just a short paddle to the top of the portage at High Falls but what a difference. The water appeared twenty feet lower, and flooded land was everywhere. Instead of an open expanse of water, with hills of pine trees in the background, there was only acres of stumps surrounded by marsh and muddy pools. With the low water there was of course quite a hill from the waters edge to the beginning of the portage. It was quite a different spot than I recalled. There were still more new buildings, and the first cabin was being used as a storehouse. I looked on the wall, and found where Harris Whitaker and I had written our names twenty-five years ago, and it was one of the first registrations on said wall. There were many more, among them my own boys, written in nineteen-fifty. It looked like there were people around, but we did not see them. I found out later that they go out on Sunday. They were building a new fire tower. There was a fair road all the way to Cedar Lake, and the workers came and went by truck.

We camped at the foot of the rapids, and the boys fished the foot of the falls, and there seemed to be no end of small trout. Next morning we started again, but the usual good paddling to the Pearly Dam was not there. This dam too was gone, and it was a very twisted route on very low water. We made the dam at the lower end of the Pearly marsh early in the afternoon, and as it looked like rain we decided to camp there. This part was new to all of us, and we did not know what lay between us and Cedar Lake.

We had seen much evidence of fishermen and campers all along the river, but more from here to the lake. There were signs of some very large parties, and we did not expect to get many fish the rest of the way. However, we had no trouble making Cedar Lake by lunch time, and while Jim and I were having a shave and changing our shirts, the boys caught a very nice bunch of fish. The worms had been used up for sometime, but the boys used small spinners with great success.

It was quite a paddle across Cedar Lake. When we left the mouth of the river it was fairly calm, but partways across the lake a wind came up, and I was afraid several times that the fifteen foot canoe would not make it. But outside of taking in some water, all was well. We caught the train for North Bay that night, and finished our trip with several days at Butt Lake.

Two years later Stan Groom and I made the same trip with two fishermen from Baltimore. This was in late May and early June. We had expected the flies and mosquitoes would be bad, and were not disappointed. We did not have to look for portages, and made our camp the first night at the old Paxton Dam. The water was much better than on the trip with the Kelly's, and we made good time, with just two people in each canoe. We caught as many fish as we wanted, and returned many more. This in spite of all the signs of previous fishermen. We saw quite a few deer, and many moose, mostly bulls, some with a very heavy spread, even for June. We saw some cows with calves, and at one place on Whiskey Jack a cow with twins.

We had planned a side trip to Whiskey Jack and Robinson Lakes. The portage from High Falls is about two miles, but we took nothing but the canoes and tackle. The trip was spoiled by some heavy rain showers, but we had good fishing, both for speckled and lake trout.

I mentioned that we had trouble with blackflies and mosquitoes. It was not as bad as we had feared, as we used plenty of spray and repellent, but the last mile on the river, before we reached the portage that would take us into Cedar Lake, there were blackflies such as I had never seen. We were on a wide stretch of the river with the usual stumps and marsh, left when the dam ceased to hold water, and there was a good breeze, but there were blackflies. As we paddled there were times it felt like someone was pelting us with fine grain, and when we got ashore there was hardly a spot of exposed skin that did not have a bite. We attempted to have a meal at the water's edge when we got to Cedar Lake, but the clouds of blackflies, plus a few mosquitoes made it impossible. We did find a point well out in the lake where heavy winds kept the bugs at a minimum.

On this trip we saw signs of many fishing parties. There had been fishermen even at the foot of the Paxton Dam. Then below the bridge, above where Lature Creek joins the river, it looked like there had been many parties. We were early enough so that we had good fishing at all the dams and usual fishing spots. We did not see any other parties, or any Rangers during the entire trip.

With all the old dams gone, and the stream back to its pre-dam level, the going on the river was sometimes very slow, as it meant many long paddles to cover short distances. Anyone who has travelled winding streams knows how it is when you have to paddle so far to get only a short distance.

I recall on the first trip I made on the Nipissing, the marshy stretch just below Dougay's Camp. The improvement crew were doing some work on it as we came along, and we got out of the canoe to take a look. Pete Mayhew explained there was a long stretch that almost made a circle and they had hoped to speed up the log drive by making a short cut. In the spring, the floods made the water much higher. So a boom was placed across the river, and the logs urged by the water and manpower to take the new course. Just for the fun I paced the distance from water to water, and it was just thirty-two paces. As we had plenty of time we paddled around and even with the help of a bit of current, it took us twenty-eight minutes to get that far by canoe.

The Nipissing River has for some reason or other many natural springs along its banks. Perhaps other waters do too, but they're more noticeable on this particular waterway. This perhaps accounts for the many pools we found that had speckled trout. I had been told by my father about a good spot to fish. This was a bit of a lake in the marsh, near the head of the flood caused by High Dam. The pond or lake covers perhaps three acres, and was known to the old timers as a place where speckled trout congregate. Only the last time I was there did any of my fishermen try it, and we caught only coarse fish, mostly perch. It was mid-day and we were using flies and small spinners. There are perhaps several springs feeding it, and the water is kept cool.

I mentioned that on the first trip with Mr. Folsom we carried from Roseberry Lake to Lature Creek, and paddled down into the river. I had taken a load across the afternoon before we took off for the river. The portage was along the old tote road for almost its entire length and the going was good. The area had not reforested itself following a fire fifteen years before, and it was quite open. There are two or three shallow lakes or ponds in a depression east of the portage and, on the return trip, I was thirsty and went down to see if I could find a drink. I expected the water to be warm, as there was no shade whatever. Imagine to my surprise to find several springs feeding these ponds. The water was cool clear and very good for drinking. Looking from shore it did not appear that there was more than two or three feet of water in these ponds.

Crow River

More than half a century ago, many fishermen and campers wanted to fish the Crow River. Back when it was well hidden in the woods. There was no trail from Opeongo, and it took several days travelling to get to Crow Lake. Today it is well-known, and many people do fish there.

The stream known as the Crow River takes the flow from Crow and the lakes above it to Lake Lavielle*. The stream is not large, and many dams and side piers show that numerous logs have been driven down its entire length. The dams and other small falls create pools, which make splendid harbours for speckled trout. There must be many cold springs along the banks, for this is one stream where the trout seemed to stay all summer. I imagine that recent fishing pressure has taken its toll, but at one time you could always be sure of getting speckled trout in Crow River.

The thing that was most noticeable as you reached the first dam was the old lumber camps. These camps were built and used by McLaughlin Brothers, and are perhaps the largest set of camps, or were, in Algonquin Park. When I first saw them they had been in use only a few years before, and they were in good condition. It is quite likely that they are all fallen in by now.

The camps were constructed of logs, as were all of the camps in those days. Camps usually consisted of the sleep camp, the cookery, the offices, the teamster's camp, the blacksmith shop and perhaps a storehouse. Teamsters had their own sleep camp, as their hours were a bit different from the other workers, as they had to arise earlier in the morning to feed their horses, and sometimes they were later at night, especially when the log haul was on. At

---

*Lake Lavielle — named for the geographer accompanying explorer Samuel de Champlain

this camp they must have had two of everything except the office and blacksmith shop. I never took the trouble to count how many logs had been used in the construction of the buildings, but if they had been piled in a lumber yard, they would have made many piles of lumber. Today it seems such a waste to use so many logs in buildings, but these were nearly all red pine, which did not have much value in those days.

It was near his little camp close to the first dam on the river that I initially met Leonard Turcotte. Leonard was the Fire Ranger there, and had been for many years. He later moved to Eagle or Butt Lake, then to Park Headquarters and has now been retired for several years. He is perhaps the oldest living person to have spent most of his adult life in Algonquin Park.

The Crow River is not a very large or fast stream. Navigable most of the way, there are, nevertheless, some portages. These can be *run* in the spring when the water is high, but in the summer they must be portaged. Fishermen have to wade when fishing, but as I recall it, there are many pools and deep holes that always produce trout. The scenery is also very pleasant, and it is on the lower section of the river that a good stand of jack pine can be noted. This type of pine does not appear to grow in all sections of the Park.

There is a noticeable drop in the River about halfway down. The portage is not long, and passes through a stand of second growth pine. I always enjoyed camping there and found it was not hard to get enough fish for supper. The noise of the water going over and around the rocks, plus the slight breezes through the pine tops, always made for a restful sleep. On this particular spot, I have proved to many that it is much more restful sleeping alongside a stream if you lie with your feet downstream. The scientists have a theory, something to do with currents, which may or may not be right, but I do know that you get a much better rest when camping by a river if you lie with your feet down stream. Try it sometime and you will see. If you are camping where there is no current in the water, sleep with your head to the north.

Crow River makes a very quiet entrance into Lavielle. This is one of the larger lakes, and has produced many fish. Unlike many of the other larger lakes, this one appears to be deep, and the fishing is still as good as can be found in the Park. Since flying in was stopped, angling has improved and the lake will no doubt be a good fish producer for years.

From Lavielle the rest of the way to Petawawa the stream is known as White Partridge Creek, though the creek from that lake does not enter until further downstream. Anyone who has been fortunate enough to read 'The Incomplete Angler', has had a good description of the river. But in spite of Author Robinson's description of his trip, I would hesitate to send any of my friends there in fly season.

As a boy, I had heard of Crow Lake many times. My Dad had a trapping camp there when he was twenty, which was five years before the Park was established. His camp was on the highest point on the right hand side, just as you enter the river. The first time I had a chance I went looking for it, but I could not find anything that seemed like the remains of a camp. In all, I only found a few stones that might have been the remains of the fireplace.

When I was there in the spring of 1927, Tom Salmon showed me a white birch tree that he had been watching for years. It was then perhaps a foot in diameter, and was a perfect specimen. Tom had hoped the tree would be large enough to supply bark for a canoe. In showing it to me, Salmon was hopeful that when the tree grew a couple of inches more, I would make good use of it, and build a bark canoe.

I did not see that birch again for years. When we were on Crow Lake in 1946, travelling the old McLaughlin, I went to see the tree and as we were travelling light thought it possible to take it out. The tree was still there, but it had been ringed by beaver, and had been dead a couple of years. I will always feel that I betrayed a trust, for Tom fervently hoped someone would have a canoe out of the tree he had been watching for so many years.

The Tim River (Pine River)

The river that is now called the *Tim River* was ordinarily called the Pine River. Many of the older people still refer to it as the Pine River. The name, of course, was applicable because of the great stands of pine that were so evident along its full length. Perhaps the only other so-called river with so many pines along its banks was the Nipissing River, which runs in the same general direction, as both are tributaries of the Petawawa.

The Tim really get its start outside the boundaries of Algonquin Park, on the western border. Where it enters the Park, it is only a creek, but soon it hits the marsh that continues to Tim's Lake, and from a point just inside the Park it is navigable.

I have not been able to determine when the lake was first called Tims Lake. Many of the real early woodsmen knew it as Shoe Lake because of the resemblance in shape to that of a shoe. Some say it was named after Tim O'Leary, the first Chief Ranger, others after Tim Holland, one of the early hunters and the man who had the camp at Butt Lake.

Booths had a camp on Tims Lake before the turn of the century. The foreman was a man of French descent, named Valenquette. The clearing where his camp was located was easily found on my first visit. This was what was called a timber camp, as they cut and hauled only square timber. If a tree showed any sign of defect it was passed by, and there are many large pine still lying on the ground, as they were not of the quality required for square timber.

The history of square timber is an important part of our past. Logs were 'squared' in the woods by men using heavy broad axes. They were then hauled to the nearest river, floated or driven down to the nearest railroad, all the way to Georgian Bay. In the early days, timber was hauled all the way from the head of Long Lake, then upstream to Tims Lake. This meant a lift over the falls which are a few miles below Tims Lake. When I made my first trip to Tims Lake, in 1917, this lift or bridge was still standing. It was constructed of heavy timber, and was perhaps two hundred feet long. From Tims Lake the road continued on up stream to a point not far outside the Park. The sleighs were then drawn uphill with a hoist operated by a steam cable, and thence down the other side of the height of land to the Magnetawan River.

In olden times, the timbers were driven all the way to Byng Inlet on the Georgian Bay. After the Canada Atlantic was built, a loading platform was constructed at Kearney and the timbers were loaded there. Most, if not all, the square timber was shipped to England. The fact it was squared, as in many cases the waine* was left on, made for easier shipping. The dealers in England and Scotland would not accept square timber that had been sawn, or made in a mill. Stories are told of one lumber company who did *square* their logs in the mill, and to insure sale had men who did nothing else but finish the work with a plane and put some axe marks on to make it appear to have been hewn in the woods.

The axe men of the early lumbering years were the elite of the workmen. The men who worked in square timber were of three classes. First, the liners, men who took off a slice of bark the whole length of the log, and marked it by using a chalk line. Next the score hacker came along and chopped and scored until he had 70% of the slab removed. Then the broad axemen hewd to the line until one side was smooth. Then the log was turned on its flat side, and the process repeated until the four sides of the log had had a slab removed.

The score hacker used a special heavy axe. Some I have seen around old camps must have weighed seven pounds. They were built with a ridge in the centre, running from near the cutting edge to the back of the axe. This ridge prevented the axe sticking.

The broad axe was the largest of all axes. I have used some that were near ten or eleven pounds. I have been told by oldtimers that some of the really good axemen used axes up to fourteen pounds.

There are many stories about the old time axemen. Most of them were experts, and some of the timbers that are in the old buildings hardly show the mark of an axe. I watched them years ago, and marvelled at how they could swing those heavy axes over their shoulders and follow a line the full length of a log, always coming down with that twelve inch blade right on the line. One old axeman told me of a broad axe contest he witnessed, when several noted axemen were contesting for the honour of best axeman in the county. There was no special rule. Each man was supposed to do what he thought was good work, and the judges were having a diffcult time trying to decide which was the best work, when one of the older men went into the house, and came out with a newspaper. He carefully opened it, pasted it on the side of one of the better hewn logs, then with a smile for the crowd picked up his axe and very carefully hewd off the print.

---

*WAINE — *similar to square timber but edges left rounded in natural curve or wane*

My first trip to Tims Lake was in October 1917, when I went in to help my Father take a stove down to the shelter hut at Roseberry Lake. We carried very little in the line of supplies, as there was a good supply at each cabin. On entering the camp, we were quite upset to see that someone had left the cupboard door open, and the mice had ruined just about all the supplies. We had no trouble catching fish, but that was all we had.

There was an incident that same day I will never forget, and one that I never told while my Father was alive. While fishing we saw two deer come in the lake, and then a wolf howled. Dad quickly headed for the camp and his rifle. Loading it, he told me to walk up the trail to the wagon road, as the wolves would travel the road. There was a branch, perhaps to get around a wet spot, where the portage trail crossed route. I decided on the second route.

In a few minutes I could hear the wolves coming, as there was little foliage, and it was very dry. Though I could not see far, I raised and cocked the rifle. The wolf pack took the first road, and of course when they came to the trail they smelled my tracks. There was quite a scramble, and one even howled a bit, or perhaps barked is better. At any rate, it made me jump, and I pulled the trigger. When I returned to camp Dad asked about the shot, and I explained the wolves were running and I could not see very well. I never did tell him I jumped when the wolves howled, and shot from nervousness.

At the time the shelter hut was on the north side of Tims Lake, near where the portage goes to the lake enroute to the east side of the lake. Later, with the Park policy changing, the shelter was burned.

Lands and Forests once built a wooden fire tower on a hill near the lake, but it has long since rotted away.

We did a lot of fishing in Tims Lake, in 1934 and 1935. We took supplies and equipment in by horse and wagon. The fishing was good, but this is another lake with not too much water, and the fishing did not last. For years there were large quantities of fish taken out and with a lumber road on the north side the lake became quite accessible.

The largest of the speckled trout any of our parties caught was in a lake just north of Tims. In 1934, we caught three, ranging in weight from four to six pounds. The next summer I fished there with a man and his wife from Jordan, Mr. and Mrs. W.E. Troupe. We caught three the first day, with a six pounder topping the catch.

Earlier I mentioned that Booths had built a dam at the foot of Long Lake in 1912. They built and improved the dams the rest of the way down the stream. There was a dam two or three miles further down water, another a mile below the Farm, and one at the foot of Shippedew Lake. When these dams were in good condition it made for very easy canoeing, as there was usually a good head of water, even in the summer. At the lower side of the dam there was usually a few speckled trout. Since the disappearance of the dams the pools they created have gone. There was also a dam, built in 1920 at the head of the falls below Tims Lake. Like the others it has long rotted away.

The farm known as the Pine River Farm, is about half way between

Roseberry Lake and Shippegew Lake. It was first used by, I believe, the Colonial Lumber Company. It was a place where the horses could be put out to pasture in the summer. The men who were left to watch planted patches of potatoes and other vegetables and perhaps raised a number of pigs. There are several such farms in Algonquin Park, though they were mostly called depots.

The original clearing at the Pine River Farm must have been over two hundred acres. It has grown in somewhat now, but there is still standing a very large clearing. The old buildings have fallen, the only one still standing is the Rangers Cabin., which was built in the late twenties from timber and lumber salvaged from some of the old buildings.

I first saw it in 1923, and at that time there had not been much canoe travelling on the river. The buildings were in good shape, as the Booth Lumber Company had repaired them, when Booth was lumbering there. The land produced fine crops of vegetables, bothered quite a bit by deer, as they seemed to be able to jump the fences, and had a liking for the fresh green things, especially turnips.

There are several very fine fishing holes along the river. These were once destroyed to a certain extent when logs were floated down to the main river. As holes and sand bars were gouged out by the drive and deposits of bark littered the sides of the stream. It was not long after the log drives had been discontinued that the fishing improved. Some of the old well-known spots produced trout again, and there is still good fishing.

In 1913 there was a bush fire that burned in the slash left from cutting logs and pulpwood. It burned a considerable area on both sides of the river, starting below the falls, and continuing down well below the farm. The resultant, fresh feed was a great drawing card for deer, and in the open places the following years, it was not uncommon to see groups of thirty deer. Travelling on the river, one could see deer at every turn. Like all other heavily populated areas, the deer left when food got scarce.

There is a spot a couple of miles below the falls where one could land a canoe and climb up a not too steep hill, finally climb up on a large rock, and get a marvelous panoramic view of a large section of woods and plains. There are a lot of burned over areas scattered around. Some of which did not reforest itself. However considerable areas exist of new growth white pine. There are no lakes, the only water visible being the river, but it is well worth the effort of climbing the hill.

Not too many years ago, three of us had an unusual experience not too far from this spot. We were camped at Eagle Lake with a group of fishermen from Orillia, three men and their wives. I had taken two of the men down to one of my favourite trout 'holes'. It was quite a trip down and back, and meant only a couple of hours fishing. This is a trip we often made, for besides the fishing there was the pleasure of river travelling, as well as game to be seen. We had a leisure lunch near a good landing, and were all packed to leave when out of the brush about fity feet away came a deer. It happened so fast we did not have time to do anything but look. The deer, a nice buck, passed between two feet of us, and we were only a few feet apart. Its sides were heaving, and while it was trying hard its jumps seemed to be very short. One of the men asked what scared the deer. I only had time to answer 'wolves' when several broke through the same underbrush. They came to a sudden stop when they saw us standing there, and made a very hasty retreat. I do not know how many there were, most likely a family of pups and their parents. I think we saw five, but there were more in the brush. The period from when we first saw the deer to when we saw the last wolf disappear was only a matter of perhaps thirty seconds, but the wolves always howl while chasing deer. I have heard several deer being killed by wolves, and there was no sound except the bleat of the deer, and a few wolf growls afterwards. I have been close many times, when wolves put deer into the water, and there wasn't any sound from the wolves.

For several years following the time that Booths logged in that area, the roads and bridges were in fair shape, and telephone lines had been strung to nearly all the Ranger cabins in the park. At this time the Fire Rangers were two different groups. It was felt that the telephone would be a help in case of a fire, and they were, but it was almost impossible to keep them in repair. Trees fell on the lines, and the phones went out of order. The greatest trouble was the moose. Many times lines disappeared, and repairmen following the wire into the woods found the remains of a moose that had tangled its antlers in the wire, and eventually died. The telephones were finally taken out, as it was hardly possible to keep them in good order.

From the farm, the usual stopping place on the river, it is a short paddle to the dam, and from there to Shippegew Lake, which is known as *The Marsh*. When water is high, it is a very nice trip, as there is usually game to be seen, and a continually changing view on the river. Shippegew is an odd lake, and does not seem to belong with the other lakes in that area. It is shallow and there are no trout in the lake. The lake marks the end of water travel, as from this lake to the next, there is a very hilly portage. Near the upper end of the portage there once stood one of the old camboose* camps, long since decayed away.

---

*camboose—fire for cooking and heating built on sand in the centre of the 19th Century shanty

The Wolf

There are a lot of people who think that there are a great many wolves in Algonquin Park. Especially since the Ministry of Natural Resources have been making a study of wolves in the Park, to see if they can find their breeding, travelling and eating habits, and any other data that would help in the control of wolves when needed. It is reasonable to expect that where there has been such a high concentration of deer for so many years that the wolves would also be there, and this is true. However, there are not as many as is generally believed, and very few are seen by travellers.

In all the seasons I have spent in Algonquin Park, not counting the wolves we saw during deer hunts, I do not think I have seen more than thirty wolves. They of course are not dangerous, as there is no record of them molesting humans. Many do not share my views, but the records speak for themselves. Only recently a leading newspaper carried an article on a search for a missing airplane, believed down in the northern portion of the Park, stating that the searchers did not want to be out in the night because of the presence of wolves. (Reports are stupid.)*

During the month of May, 1933, we had a fishing camp on Scott or Magnetawan Lake. Fishing was not too good, so four of us decided on a trip to Roseberry Lake, down the Pine River to the Falls and home by way of Queer Lake and Little Trout Lake. There were two guides and two fishermen. The other guide was Bill Laking, the fishermen — Phil Burdick, and Claude Ackerman of Friendship, New York. We travelled in one large canoe, and made very good time. This was before the populace knew of some of the best fishing holes, so we had a good catch of specks in the river. We saw plenty of

Editor's note: The comment is Ralph's.

game, mostly moose and beaver, as the deer were just showing signs of getting plentiful after being very scarce for several years. As we landed at the portage on Queer Lake the trout were rising. Everyone wanted to fish, and it was getting late. While the other three were casting, I built a fire and made a pot of tea, and dug into the pack for what was left of our noon day lunch.

I called supper, but no one seemed to be in a hurry to eat, and after taking stock of the spread, I decided there was at least a good meal for one. I was just on my second sandwich when someone called out to look at the deer swimming in the narrow part of the lake. They watched the deer, while I kept on eating. Next Phil Burdick called '*What is that behind the deer?*', and I kept on eating. It was easy to see it was a wolf and that it would catch the deer before it could get to shore.

There was not any time to make plans, so I grabbed the axe, jumped in the canoe and took after the wolf. Just as I got started I realized that I had only one paddle, but there was no time to get the other one. I managed to get between the wolf and the shore and turn it back out in the lake. As I got close I wondered just what was going to happen when I tried to kill the wolf. As I got close he or rather she made a lunge at the canoe and got a very light grip on the gunwhale. By turning the canoe up a little I made it impossible for the wolf to get it's teeth in it. I picked up the axe, but the canoe had lost some of its momentum and instead of hitting the wolf on the head, the axe came down on its shoulders. I was using the blade, and the axe went right to the handle. When the axe struck, the wolf reached around and gripped the axe handle with its teeth, and left marks that are still there. I shoved it under the water, thinking it might drown. The wolf had different ideas, and kicked loose and stuck its head out of the water again. I was ready this time, and hit it between the eyes, still using the blade. The blow finished the wolf instantly.

Of course, when we arrived at camp that night, with the trout and the wolf, it caused a lot of comment. I have hunted and trapped since I can remember. I even killed a bear with a club at the tent one morning. But I have never again experienced the excitement of that unusual battle with a wolf.

Another thing happened at that camp that I still chuckle over. This involved a large party, all Americans. Elsewhere I mentioned catching a speckled trout in Roseberry Lake with an otter in its stomach. This was the same crowd of fishermen.

As is usual in camps where there are several fishermen, there was a bet on each day for the largest and the most fish. I was top guide, and I paddled Claude Ackerman. We never seemed to get in any winning bracket, and as a result we were subject to a great deal of kidding because of our inability to fish. Ackerman was a lawyer, and during the morning I suggested that he make some bets with the crowd, make them without loopholes, and also make it on an ascending scale. Meaning that if we doubled the catch, or redoubled it the bet would increase on a like scale. I would not tell him my plan, but offered to split the bet if we lost or if we won.

After lunch I managed to get a good sized gunny sack in my pack, and we went fishing. At the eastern end of Daisy Lake there is a falls where sometimes there are a few speckled trout. At the rapids half a mile further down there are usually a few more specks. But at the foot of the falls there are often many of those big white shiner-like fish, so common all the way down the Petawawa. We did catch some nice speckled — one over three pounds, which was tops for size. Then we started to catch these big shiners. In Misty Lake I have seen them as large as three pounds, but up the river they do not get so large. We caught as many as I felt I could carry. I think we took home nearly a hundred fish. I do not recall how much we collected in bets, but the next day the new ruling was that only trout counted.

Anyone who has been in that section of Algonquin Park knows that there are several lengthy portages to get to Scott Lake. One time Dad and I had gone in ahead to set up camp, and had taken in the supplies and camp equipment. When the party got off the train next morning at Eagle Lake Landing, quite a number of boxes were put off with them, and it did not look like they intended to drink much water. These cases of beer made it necessary for at least one extra trip on the portage and would mean a lean lunch. As soon as the fishermen had disappeared we hid enough beer and one bottle of rye in a swamp, so that when we came out there would be a drink for everyone. It has been my experience that no matter how much parties take to drink, they are always dry on the last day, and this trip was no exception. The poker game the last night was not the usual hillarious affair as others had been, and by the time we had reached the last lake going out they were actually drinking water. Their joviality quickly returned when the beer was produced, and the trip ended in a very hearty manner.

Fishing Holes

The first years I guided in Algonquin Park I was told many times of good fishing holes, on lakes as well as streams. At that time all lake fishing was good, but fishing on streams in the warm weather could be spotty, and it was very handy to know where the best spots were.

Perhaps thirty years ago everyone talked about the marvelous fishing at the Glory Hole. I do not know where the name originated, but that particular location is at the upper end of what we called Hardy's Bay on Lake Lavielle, where the creek from Dixon Lake (formerly Lake Clear) emptied into Lavielle. I was there many years before the spot had acquired a name, and not too many people had fished it. In fact, I was there several times, spring and summer, and never saw signs of any other fishermen.

The most notable trip was in 1926. Six of us, four fishermen and two guides went in by way of Opeongo to Crow River. After the first few days, Tom Clarke, Manager of Highland Inn, and guide Tom Salmon, returned to Whitney, and the other four of us went on through to Lake Travers. Angling of course was good, as it was early May and there were very few flies. We were camped at the dam at the foot of Lavielle, and late one afternoon four of us went in one canoe to the top of Hardy's Bay. The fishing was fabulous. I do not recall ever seeing so many fish anxious to be caught. They were not large, only a few as heavy as two pounds, but we fished until everyone got tired of it. We kept only what we could eat right there, and I could only hazard a guess on the number we returned. We were using only two rods and took turns. Lures were any small spinner, and I think the average would be at least nine or ten casts to produce a fish.

Then there was a little pond southeast of Agnone Station, now called Lake Travers. There was a walk of at least five miles, and Mr. Folsom and I had been there the year before. If my memory is correct the pond is hardly more than three acres, and not more than ten feet deep at any spot, with eight feet being average. We fished from a raft someone else had built, and all the fish were taken by casting, with the small spinners. Again it was almost a fish for each cast, but these were small, ten inches being about as large as we caught. The fact that these trout lived in a lake or pond that was so shallow, contradicts biological claims that they need much deeper water than that to live in.

There is a good speckled trout hole on the Petawawa River about Taylor's Chute. My father told me about it years ago, and I have only fished it once, as it is out of the usual line of travel. I was there in the summer of '57, with the Kelly party, and from our start at Butt Lake kept telling them of the good fishing we could expect. The hole was still there and there were still plenty of fish, but there were three canoes tied to the brush on the shore, and six men fishing. They had found the place quite by accident, but were making good use of their find. We were a bit disappointed in seeing people there, but they gave us plenty for a good lunch, so we really saved time.

There are at least three holes on the Pine or as it is now called, the Tim River. One, just above the Pine River Farm, has provided many a good lunch or dinner. Another lays halfway between the falls and the Farm. The third is above Roseberry Lake. I was down the river in the summer of 1951 and each hole cost me a dollar. I was with Harris Whitaker, and at each spot I made the bet that I could catch enough for a meal in fifteen minutes. On most occasions this was an easy bet to win, but on this trip I did not produce a fish from any of the holes.

The best catch of speckled trout, and the easiest that has been my good luck to help take, was in 1949. I was guiding two young fellows from Hamilton, and for the first two days we had fished in a stream, as they did not believe speckled trout could be caught in lakes. They were using the usual light tackle necessary to take fish up to twelve or fourteen inches.

We arrived at Butt Lake about noon, and there was no trouble getting a laker for lunch. In the afternoon we went to Queer Lake, as I wanted to prove to the boys that specks in excess of three pounds, did live in lakes.

Many years ago my Dad told me of a great catch of speckled trout being caught where the little creek came in from Little Trout. He also told me that he had seen it only once in all the years he had been there. Queer Lake back then was one of the accepted good lakes, noted for real large fish.

When we arrived at the lake, I suggested that we try a few casts in the pool where the creek enters. There was not more than two feet of water, and the pool was not much more than sixteen by twenty feet. I suggested that heavier tackle be used, but one of the boys scoffed at the idea, claiming that he could take any trout on that tackle. After he had broken three leaders he changed to heavier ones.

I do not know how many trout we could have taken. As we had three licences, we stopped at fifteen fish, averaging two pounds, but with some over three pounds. That was the nicest catch of speckled trout I have ever seen. I have seen more, and some that were larger, but never so many of such good size.

I mention in the story of the Nipissing, about a pond just above Lature Creek that was noted years ago for speckled trout. I think perhaps the wearing out of the High Dam, thereby lowering the water by about at least 80% of its former volume, has had a bearing on the fishing on that portion of the river. At any rate, the last two times I tried fishing some of the special spots, there were very few fish around. It has been fished more heavily the last few years but it is my belief that if the dam was still holding water as it did thirty-five years ago, there would be a lot more trout.

Halfway between Proulx Lake and Little Crow, was another proven spot for small trout. One of my parties discovered this by accident. It was quite windy, and we had stopped for a breather, and one of the men threw a bit of coloured cigar wrapping into the water. Several trout came up to investigate and you can imagine the scramble to get lines assembled. We took as many as we could use, and on return visits found that we could always take enough fish for a meal.

Like speckled trout, Lake trout also seem to congregate at certain points. Just why you can drop an anchor in one location and catch lake trout, while a hundred yards away there does not appear to be any I can't explain. I know of one spot where we still fish a lot, and if the anchor location is missed by fifty feet the catch will be small.

I found a grand spot once to catch bass. All our bass are small mouth black bass. We do not have the large mouth bass. The occasion was over fifty-five years ago, and we were camped on Rock Lake, one of the good bass lakes. My brother Art and I had a party from Cleveland — two men and a boy. This particular morning Art had stayed in camp with the boy, and I took the two men to Pen Falls. It was some distance down to the falls, and the wind was very strong and against us on the way back. Just for a rest we pulled into a small bay, and one of the fishermen decided that since we were there he might as well fish. The next half hour was a riot. Seemed as though there were hundreds of bass in that little bay, and all of them hungry. I do not remember how many we took, but we did keep four, all over four pounds.

There was a station agent at Algonquin Park, Bert Needham, very well known and always asking for a bass, which he claimed was his favourite fish. I imagine when he asked for trout he had the same plea, but Mr. Brewer, one of our party, thought it would be nice to send him the four large bass. Trains were pretty regular then, and the fish were at Algonquin Park while they were still fresh. Always one for a joke, Bert had given the fish to his son, and sent him out to fish around White's Island (now Rigby's Island), with instructions to come in just at train time.

Trains came twice daily then, once from the east and once from the west. There were other trains of course, but these were the main passenger trains, and everyone from the hotel and a lot of the cottagers met the train. So just a few minutes before the train time, young Needham came in with these four bass, and it is easy to understand the excitement it aroused. Next day we came back to the hotel on the same train, and there were still about a dozen boats and canoes fishing around in the area in which the fish were supposed to have been caught.

There was another spot on the same Rock Lake that produced many bass over the years. For several years we had fished with a group of American railroad people, who had their private car put on the siding at Rock Lake Station. The guides had their own camp, a nice set up, as there was no camp work to do. The party was composed of two men and their wives, and their own cook-butler, and we had only to look after ourselves. The cook was very generous too, especially when we sent in the fish well cleaned.

There was an agent there then by the name of Billy McCort. Once when fishing was not too good he suggested that we go right to the foot of the lake and fish in the pool just above the old dam. In the early twenties the old lumbering dams were in good shape, and still held some water. Billy told us he had caught many bass there, but the supply was limited.

One summer the beavers had a house in the narrows on Rain Lake. This beaver house had been abandoned and rebuilt several times, but this year, 1923, it contained a larger than usual colony. As a result there was quite a bit of brush, mixed in with the remains of the winter food pile. Whether this collection of brush was responsible or not, it did seem that the bass, particularly the large ones, kept coming to this beaver house all summer. I believe it was the Reverend Bruen who first discovered it, but afterwards my parties took many large bass at that spot. Once, fishing with Devitt, Lepage and Folsom, we took the limit back to the hotel, and the largest six weighed over thirty pounds.

There was a spot on Sawyer Lake where you could always catch two or three bass, but seldom more. Beneath three fairly good sized birch trees that grew on such a slant that their branches were just above the water, I almost always discovered two or three bass. Perhaps it was the shade, or perhaps the low branches of the trees put food into the water. I do know that since the trees have gone, and despite the fact there is still plenty of bass in the lake, they do not hang around that spot as they did when the trees were there.

Obviously fishing holes change from year to year. Especially when they become generally known and the fishing pressure gets heavier. Perhaps the best known Park pool of all was Salmon's pool, on the Oxtongue River, below Whiskey Falls. This pool was named after Tom Salmon, one of the very old and famous guides of his day. When the road was being constructed, a camp was built right near the pool and the inevitable happened. From being one of the landmarks on the river, no one ever hears it mentioned now.

There are many more fishing holes of course, and it is quite in order that some should be kept secret. This is a hard thing to do in this age of quick communication, but it's doubtful if the fishermen of fifty years hence will know of the spots where the people of my age caught fish.

Editor's Epilogue

It seems altogether appropriate to leave Ralph Bice in his beloved Algonquin Park, wetting a line in some of his favorite fishing holes. Obviously this is only a small part of his prolific writings related to the out-of-doors. At eighty years of age, Ralph continues to peck out his weekly column, *'Along the Trail'*, to the delight of readers of the *Almaguin News and The Hunstville Forester*.

Because of space limitations, it was not feasible to include in this book all the material Ralph provided. Ralph wanted the inclusion of many other friends of the Park and we are sorry that this was not possible to do.

Readers may be surprised that a book devoted to Algonquin Park had so little mention of the artist, Tom Thomson. Though appreciative of Thomson's talent as an artist, Ralph nonetheless shares the view of other Park veterans, who feel the artist's short tenure in the Park has perhaps received enough mention in other publications. It was Ralph's wish to recognize the lesser known figures associated with Ontario's oldest Provincial Park.

Barry Penhale

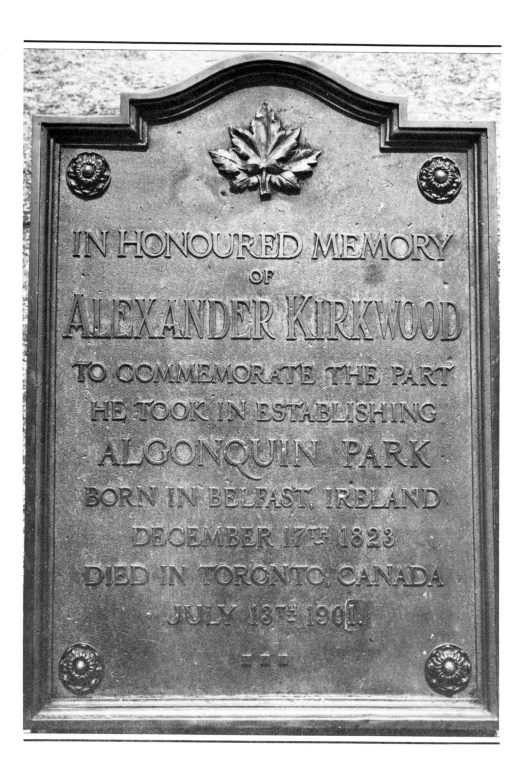

IN HONOURED MEMORY
OF
ALEXANDER KIRKWOOD
TO COMMEMORATE THE PART
HE TOOK IN ESTABLISHING
ALGONQUIN PARK
BORN IN BELFAST, IRELAND
DECEMBER 17TH 1823
DIED IN TORONTO, CANADA
JULY 13TH 1901.

References

For further reading about Algonquin Park history,
we recommend the following books:

EARLY DAYS IN ALGONQUIN PARK
by Ottelyn Addison, 1974
McGraw-Hill Ryerson
Toronto/ 144 pp

ALGONQUIN STORY
by Audrey Saunders, 1963
Ontario Dept. of Lands & Forests
Toronto/ 196 pp

TOM THOMSON — THE ALGONQUIN YEARS
by Ottelyn Addison, with Elizabeth
Harwood, 1969, The Ryerson Press
Toronto/ 98 pp

TOM THOMSON
by Blodwen Davies, 1967
Mitchell Press Ltd.
Vancouver/ 102 pp

HURLING DOWN THE PINE
by John W. Hughson & Courtney C.J.
Bond, 1964, The Historical Society of
the Gatineau, Old Chelsea
Quebec/ 130 pp

A HUNDRED YEARS A-FELLIN'
by Charlotte Whitton, 1974
The Runge Press, Ltd.
Ottawa / 172 pp

PRINGROVE THROUGH THE YEARS
by Edmund H. Kase, Jr., 1975
(published by the author) / 237 pp

JACK GERVAIS — RANGER AND FRIEND
by Edmund H. Kase, Jr., 1970
(published by the author) / 61 pp

CAMPING IN THE MUSKOKA REGION — A STORY
ABOUT ALGONQUIN PARK
by James Dickson, 1960
Ontario Dept. of Lands and Forests
Toronto / 164 pp

A HISTORY OF PEMBROKE FOREST DISTRICT
NO. 21,
District History Series, 1967
Ontario Dept. of Lands and Forests
Toronto / 42 pp

EARLY DAYS IN HALIBURTON
by H.R. Cummings, 1962
Ontario Dept. of Lands & Forests
Toronto / 42 pp

THE UPPER OTTAWA VALLEY
by Clyde C. Kennedy, 1970
Renfrew County Council
Pembroke
Ontario / 256 pp

GREAT BRITAIN'S WOODYARD
by Arthur R.M. Lower, 1973
McGill-Queen's University Press
Montreal / 271 pp

RENEWING NATURE'S WEALTH
by Richard S. Lambert, with Paul
Pross, 1967, Ontario Dept. of
Lands & Forests
Toronto / 630 pp

ACKNOWLEDGEMENTS

thankyou

Edna Bice for sharing Ralph with us.
Peggy Sochasky, Nancy Penhale and Heather Wakeling for typing.
Elizabeth Parker and Marc Solomon for editorial and proof reading assistance.

PHOTOGRAPHIC CREDITS
Miss Miriam Folsom / Members of the Pitt Family / Helen McGregor
Mary (Colson) Clare / Aubrey Dunn / Mrs. Ed Sawyer / Dr. James Devitt
Rose Thomas / Al Newell / G.B. Hayes / Mrs. William Mooney
Almaguin News / Ministry of Natural Resources

Design by John Elphick

Production by Marc Solomon

Typesetting by Jean Denison & Ella Alexander
at Erin Graphics

Lithography by Maracle Press

COVER PHOTOS

Pine River, 1943
Ralph guiding Mr. and Mrs. Bill Findlay.

C. P. Folsom and Ralph with a Rain Lake catch — 1922 style.
Folsom first came to the Park in 1912 and made his last trip from Dayton, Ohio,
in 85th year.

Rangers Tim O'Leary and Steve Waters on patrol, 1897.

Rock Lake Station Circa 1914-15.

Men of the woods at work.

Jack Eastaugh at work.

Jack Eastaugh/ Carver and Painter

It is most fitting that the illustrations contained in Along the Trail are the work of a multi-talented Canadian, whose own intimate knowledge of Algonquin Park spans more than 40 years.

Eastaugh has been associated with the Taylor Statten Camps in Algonquin Provincial Park, since 1939. An expert artist and carver of totem poles, masks and plaques, the retired educator spends each summer in the Park and is considered Algonquin's Artist-in-residence.

Jack's paddling ability and some resemblance to the painter Tom Thomson (1877-1917), resulted in his portraying Thomson on CBC television.